SEEDS *OF* DISCORD

*New Mexico
in the aftermath of the
American Conquest, 1846–1861*

SEEDS *OF* DISCORD

*New Mexico
in the aftermath of the
American Conquest, 1846-1861*

Alvin R. Sunseri

Nelson-Hall nh Chicago

Library of Congress Cataloging in Publication Data

Sunseri, Alvin R.
   Seeds of discord.

   Bibliography: p.
   Includes index.
   1. New Mexico— History—1848.
2. Mexican Americans—New Mexico—History.
I. Title.
F801.S9   978.9'04   78-24315
ISBN 0-88229-141-6

Manufactured in the United States of America

10   9   8   7   6   5   4   3   2   1

Contents

Acknowledgments

In the preparation of this book I have drawn upon the ideas, suggestions, and services of many individuals. Included among these are: Karl Wittfogel for the idea that led to the examination of the irrigation system in New Mexico; Burl Noggle for the historiographical and bibliographical knowledge provided in his article dealing with Anglo observers of the Spanish borderlands; Myra Ellen Jenkins, New Mexico State Historian, for her research assistance and criticisms that have been most constructive; T. Harry Williams for the influence he has had in shaping my career both as a teacher and researcher; Gordon Rhum who in his role as Dean of the Graduate College at the University of Northern Iowa provided me with much of the support I needed to complete my research; also I wish to thank Linda Petersen and Mary Kay Ellis for their assistance in editing the manuscript. In addition, I want to express my gratitude for the help provided me by the staff and faculty in the following departments at the University of Northern Iowa: the Word Processing Center; the Social Research Center; the Readers Services Department and Interlibrary Loan Service; and the Department of History. However, whatever faults may be found with this work are solely my responsibility. Acknowledgment must also be given to the following journals to reprint versions of articles that appeared in their publications: Section I of

Chapter 2: *Agricultural History*, October 1973; Section II of Chapter 2: *El Palacio* (P. O. Box 2087, Santa Fe, New Mexico), Spring 1976; Section III of Chapter 2: *El Palacio*, Spring 1977; Chapter 5: *El Palacio*, Fall 1975; Section IV of Chapter 8: *Negro History Bulletin*, November 1975; Section III of Chapter 4: *Indian Historian*, November 1973; Section I of Chapter 7: *Journal of Mexican-American History*, December 1973.

Chronology

1535—

Cabeza de Vaca and the survivors of an ill-fated expedition, including Estevan the Moor, crossed the southern part of New Mexico. Estevan returned as a guide for a group searching for the Seven Cities of Cibola in 1539. He was killed by disgruntled natives.

1546—

Francisco Coronado led his expedition into New Mexico. They found no cities with riches but only hostile Indians who had to be subdued. Interest in the possibility of riches in New Mexico continued to dominate Spanish minds in the sixteenth century.

1598—

Don Juan de Onate commenced the settlement of New Mexico in 1598 (ten years before Jamestown was settled) and established the first capital at San Juan Pueblo.

1610—

Santa Fe, the oldest state capital in the United States, founded.

1680—

Pueblo Indians, reputedly under the leadership of Pope (a San Juan Indian living at Taos), revolted, killed over four hundred Spaniards, and drove the remainder from New Mexico.

1692—

Don Diego de Vargas, employing a keen sense of diplomacy, reestablished Spanish control of New Mexico. The following year he led eight hundred Spanish colonists to Santa Fe.

1706—

Albuquerque, the largest city in New Mexico today, founded.

1725—

First annual fair at Taos was held.

1770-1780—

The times of troubles in New Mexico. A three-year drought was followed by an outbreak of smallpox.

1807—

Lt. Zebulon M. Pike and his American army expedition arrested by the Spaniards after entering New Mexico. They were later sent to Chihuahua and ultimately released.

1812—

Don Pedro Bautista Pino selected as deputy to the Spanish Cortes. He served in Spain for two years before returning to New Mexico after presenting a historically valuable memorial summarizing conditions in New Mexico to the king.

1821—

Signing of the Treaty of Cordova granting independence to the Spanish-American colonies. New Mexico became part of the Mexican Republic.

The first wagon train from Missouri led by William Becknell entered Santa Fe in the fall of 1821. The era of the famous Santa Fe Trail from Independence, Missouri, began.

1834—

First newspaper in New Mexico published at Santa Fe: *El Crepusculo de la Libertad*.

1837—

A large group of Pueblo Indians and Mexican-Americans, disgruntled by the threats of taxation, staged a revolt and killed Governor Albino Perez. After a period of turmoil, Manuel Armijo seized the government.

1841—

A Texas army, claiming the land as far as the Rio Grande, invaded New Mexico. They were defeated by Armijo and sent to Mexico in chains. However, the fear of conquest by Texans or Americans remained.

1846—

The United States declared war on Mexico, May 10, 1846. Brigadier General Stephen Watts Kearny led the Army of the West to Santa Fe and took possession of the territory.

1847—

The Taos Indians revolted and killed both Anglo and Hispano officials including Governor Charles Bent.

1848—

The Treaty of Guadalupe Hidalgo was signed, officially transferring New Mexico and California to the United States, and ending the Mexican War.

1850—

The Compromise of 1850 was signed. The United States government paid Texas ten million dollars to relinquish its claim to eastern New Mexico. Other provisions included the use of popular sovereignty as a means of determining the question of expansion of slavery into the territories.

1851—

Bishop Jean Baptiste Lamy arrived in New Mexico.

1853—

The United States government paid Mexico ten million dollars for the Gadsden Strip that included a large tract which is now southern and southeastern New Mexico.

1861—

New Mexico reduced in size by the formation of the Colorado Territory that included the San Luis Valley.

1862—

Battle of Glorieta Pass ("The Gettysburg of the West"). In this engagement the Union forces turned back the Confederates and perhaps prevented Southern control over the Southwest.

1862-1864—

Apache and Navaho Indians were defeated by U.S. army and New Mexican militia units and placed on the reservation at Bosque Redondo. After suffering from hunger and disease, the Navahos were released to return to their tribal homeland in the Four Corners area in 1867.

1876-1878—

Lincoln County Range War between rival cattle and banking interests. Billy the Kid (William Bonney) was one of the more notorious participants.

1880s—

Extensive railroad construction.

1891—

Free public education law was passed by the legislature.

1906—

People of New Mexico and Arizona voted on issue of Joint Statehood. New Mexico approved the measure but Arizona opposed the proposal.

1911—

Congress passed act admitting New Mexico into the Union as a state. President Taft approved the act in 1912.

1916—

Pancho Villa, Mexican revolutionary leader, attacked the town of Columbus, New Mexico. American forces unsuccessfully pursued him in his flight to northern Mexico.

1922—

Important oil discoveries made in New Mexico.

1930—

Carlsbad Caverns National Park established.

1945—

First atomic bomb exploded at Trinity Flats near Alamogordo.

1960—

350th Anniversary of founding of Santa Fe.

1967—

Beginnings of activities of the militant *Alianza* led by Reies Lopez Tijerina.

1970—

Serious disturbances on various campuses including New Mexico Highlands University and University of New Mexico. Riots were outgrowths of anti-Vietnamese War sentiments and racial as well as ethnic tensions.

1974—

The first Mexican-American since 1920, Jerry Apadoca, elected governor of New Mexico.

Preface

I

Although not as publicized as the revolt of the blacks, the waves of protests during the past decade by Mexican-Americans are belated witness to their discontent. Led by men like Cesar Chavez, Rodolfo "Corky" Gonzales and, until recently, Reies Lopez Tijerina, these people are now rejecting the second-class citizenship that has been their lot since the American conquest of New Mexico in 1846 during the Mexican War.*

The results of the work of these controversial figures, along with the less colorful contributions of others, have been manifold. Chavez, who has survived brutal attacks from both the camps of big business and the Teamster's Union, has emerged as much a champion of the oppressed as the late Martin Luther King. Gonzales, who is regarded by some Anglos as a barrio thug, has performed the almost miraculous act of forcing Anglos to pay heed to the plight of the Mexican-Americans in the barrios of Denver and the Southwest. Tijerina's impact, before he became enmeshed in a world of religious fantasy, was so devastating as to arouse in younger Mexican-Americans a spirit of reinvigorated la raza that will not run its full course until real conditions of equality are guaranteed for the Chicanos in New Mexico and West Texas.

---

*The Treaty of Guadalupe Hidalgo, which allowed Mexico fifteen million dollars' payment for New Mexico and California, was forced on the Mexican government and formalized the American conquest and occupation.

Finally, Jose Guitierez has organized a formidable alliance of Chicanos in Southwest Texas that is possessed of a great amount of political clout.

There are many manifestations of this phenomenon of change for which these men are primarily responsible. A great number of Hispanos occupy legislative, judicial, and executive posts on the national, state, and local levels. For example, New Mexico has a Mexican-American governor, Jerry Apodaca, only the third since it became a state in 1912.* Moreover, the names of Anaya, Martinez, Lujan, and Montoya are included along with those who bear Anglo surnames as members of the state administration. New Mexico also has one Mexican-American congressman, Manuel Lujan, and a non-Anglo senator, Pete Domenici, who is an Italian-American. (The late Joseph M. Montoya, a long-time U.S. senator who lost his seat in 1976, was a Mexican-American.) Despite these gains there is yet a great amount of work to be done. Lip service to minority rights is still the standard operating procedure as far as the system of justice is concerned in New Mexico. The same kind of discrimination that characterized Mexican-American history before the sixties is sometimes only too apparent. The prospects for the future, however, are much brighter than in the past.

II

This book is concerned with the origins of but one aspect of the phenomenon of Mexican-American history—the relations between the Anglo-Americans and the Mexican-Americans in New Mexico in the aftermath of the American occupation. For it is in this region that the fears and prejudices, the tensions and anxieties which characterize the conflict in the Southwest today first became, and remain, apparent on a large scale.

My interest in the plight of depressed peoples such as the Mexican-Americans dates back to my childhood when as a Sicilian-

---

*Ezequiel C. De Baca was elected governor in 1916, but died seven weeks later without occupying the office. Octaviano Larrazolo served as governor from 1919–1920.

American Catholic I was thrust into a rural Louisiana Protestant environment. As a native of New Orleans, I had never encountered anti-Dago prejudice until my family moved to a little town north of Lake Pontchartrain. I will never forget, for example, my teacher asking one day following the Italo-Ethiopian War, "Alvin, why weren't you Dagoes able to beat those Niggahs?" It was an immediate invitation for every little WASP in class to have a go at me during recess. One consequence was that even at this early date my interest in the plight of the black man was aroused, as I was perceptive enough to realize that he was the only one who occupied a lower rung on the social ladder in Louisiana than the Sicilian-American.

I continued to note these instances of prejudice for eight years in the army where, in addition to other duties, I served as an integration officer. Following my return to Louisiana, I was so disturbed by continued conditions of inequality that I left the state in 1956 and embarked upon a teaching career in New Mexico. There I remained for eight years before returning to Louisiana State University in 1963 to resume graduate work towards my Ph.D. I then accepted another teaching position in southern Colorado and continued to observe the conditions of cultural interplay in New Mexico.

III

From the very beginning of my stay in New Mexico, I was shocked by the conditions of the masses of Mexican-Americans and Indians. The bigotry and prejudice directed at them by the Anglos equaled that encountered by blacks in the South and other parts of the country. Unforgotten is the time when the Mexican-American track team, which I coached, had to travel two hundred miles through west Texas and eastern New Mexico before finding restaurant and motel owners who would offer food and bed. Neither was it possible to ignore the scenes of grinding poverty and the instances of human misery in the barrios (ghettos) of Albuquerque, the Agua Fria district of Santa Fe, and the rural regions of San Miguel and Mora counties.

In addition, my historical curiosity was sufficiently aroused by these scenes of distress to prompt me to employ my discipline in an effort to relieve that curiosity and answer the questions that continued to plague me. Why are cultural cleavages of such an extreme nature present in this serene geographic setting that deserves to be characterized by social harmony? What were the origins of these instances of grim social injustice and subsequent economic inequality that had resulted in such human misery? Can the historian employing the concepts and tools of his craft discover the answers to these questions? And if so, is it possible to gain a comprehension of the past so as to enable one to better understand the present problem in New Mexico? Finally, would greater knowledge develop the comprehension so essential to the resolution of the present problem of social conflict between the Anglo and the Mexican-American?

To me the importance of these questions is indisputable, with the last two of particular significance not only to the study of the social cleavages in New Mexico but, equally important, to the basic worth of history as a discipline. Particularly does this statement answer the attacks being leveled against the discipline by the "new barbarians" who seek only "relevancy," and by those behavioral scientists who are inclined to condemn traditional methodology and goals in favor of the marriage of history to mathematics with its emphasis on quantitative measurement.

Therefore, as the decade of the sixties emerged I became engrossed in the situation in New Mexico both as a political activist and historian. By 1963 I was aware of a certain militancy beginning to emerge among the Mexican-Americans who were rejecting the inferior status that had been imposed on them since the American occupation. Among the leaders of this movement were Clark Knowlton, then a professor of sociology at New Mexico Highlands University, and prominent, albeit controversial, figures such as "Tiny" Martinez, sometime District Attorney of San Miguel County.

While I was pleased with this protest movement, I could not help but ask myself further questions. Why so long? Why was it not until the fifth generation that the sleeping giant was aroused? Why was it not before a full century of inequality had passed that the rebellion of the Chicanos took place? Aside from the blacks and

Indians, other ethnic groups had gained social, economic, and political equality by the second or third generations. It was with these questions in mind that I conducted this examination of mid–nineteenth-century New Mexico in which I describe the relations between Mexican-Americans and Anglo-Americans as well as the social and economic environment of New Mexico, in the period immediately following the conquest and annexation of the territory by the United States. Though the general treatment is with the cultural crisis immediately following the occupation, always implicit is a concern with the problem of ethnic controversy that yet exists in the Southwest. I believe that this conflict between Mexican-Americans and Anglo-Americans has its roots in the Anglo belief that the cultural confrontation represented a contest between "barbarism and civilization." These "alien and inferior people" had to conform to the Anglo concept of progressive development if they were to be successfully incorporated into the "American system" and not remain "foreigners." The Mexican-Americans resisted the changes and failed to live up to Anglo expectations. Hence, the Anglo-Americans, and those Hispanos who desired to retain their positions of power, felt justified in treating Mexican-Americans as second-class citizens—a condition that has persisted to the present day.

I realize my deliberate choice of self-involvement with my subject will offend both the Rankean traditionalists and the new historians who seek objectivity in the computer. However, as Jessie Bernard noted in a recent work (*The Future of Marriage* [New York, 1972], p. 293), radical scholars "are now forcing us to recognize that a value judgement is implicit in the choice of any research topic. . . ." Moreover, it is my belief that content analysis of any work reveals as much knowledge about the framework within which the historian is writing as the subject of his work. Consequently, it is my hope that the following essays will not only shed more light on the period in which the seeds of discord between Hispanos and Anglos were planted, but also more clearly elucidate the spirit of the times in which they were written.

PART I
THE LAND

The Land of the Great River

Physical Features, Size and Boundaries

New Mexico is officially and popularly known as the "Land of Enchantment." It might also be styled the land of geographic and scenic contrast, for within its boundaries one encounters every form of geographic configuration and pictorial setting; from the barren plains and deserts that fill so much of the country to the majestic mountains and challenging cliffs of Frijoles Canyon; from the eerie White Sands in the south to the breathtakingly beautiful sea of grass that is La Valle Grande in the north. One can experience no lovelier view than that witnessed in Santa Fe, "the city different," during the last hour of each day as the sun reflects a roseate scene against the Sangre de Cristo Mountains to the east in which vermilion, garnet, ruby, and gold are so gloriously blended. The colorful plaza in the center of the city, forming the western terminus of the Santa Fe Trail, must have appeared as a secular millennium to the traders after the hazardous journey across the plains of Kansas and eastern Colorado into northeastern New Mexico.

The valley in which the city is located averages seven thousand feet in elevation with the surrounding snow-capped mountains rising another three to six thousand feet above sea level. Streams are fed by the rivulets carrying the melting snow from the peaks.

New Mexico, since the admission of Alaska, ranks in size as the fifth largest state in the Union. However, as large as the state is now—it is a full day's journey by car from the northeastern corner to Silver City in the southwest—far greater was the size of the territory created by Congress in the Organic Act that was part of the compromise legislation of 1850. It measured some 240,000 square miles. Moreover, at that time it took much longer to travel distances. Fifteen days were required to make the journey from Santa Fe to the Gila country within which Silver City is located today. (See map, Territory of New Mexico, 1851–1861.)

From the coming of the first conquistador in the sixteenth century to the post–Civil War period, New Mexico remained the most remote and inaccessible of the areas penetrated by both Spaniards and Anglo-Americans. There were two reasons for this lack of access: first, the territory was surrounded by mountains to the north, prairies measuring more than six hundred miles to the east, and arid lands and deserts to the south and west; second, the lands were occupied by hostile Indians who were disposed to attack those attempting to enter or leave the territory. In truth it was a land of many Indian frontiers: the Jicarilla Apache frontier to the northeast; the Comanche frontier to the east; the Mescalero, Lipan, and Gila Apache frontiers to the southeast and south; the line of Chiricahua to the southwest; the Navaho frontier to the west; and finally, the Ute frontier to the north.

This isolation, combined with the Indian menace, posed major continuing problems for the government. The most immediate one facing the administration at Washington following New Mexico's absorption in 1848, however, was the problem of a line of demarcation separating the territory from Texas. As every student of the sectional controversy is aware, this question of a boundary line continued to plague politicians during the ensuing years as the Texas problem was not resolved until the working out of the Compromise of 1850. In fact, leading figures were hazy about boundaries in any given direction. In 1853, for example, William Carr Lane, incoming governor, confessed his ignorance in a letter to his wife: "We do not know, with certainty, where the eastern boundary of the Territory runs across the road to Independence;

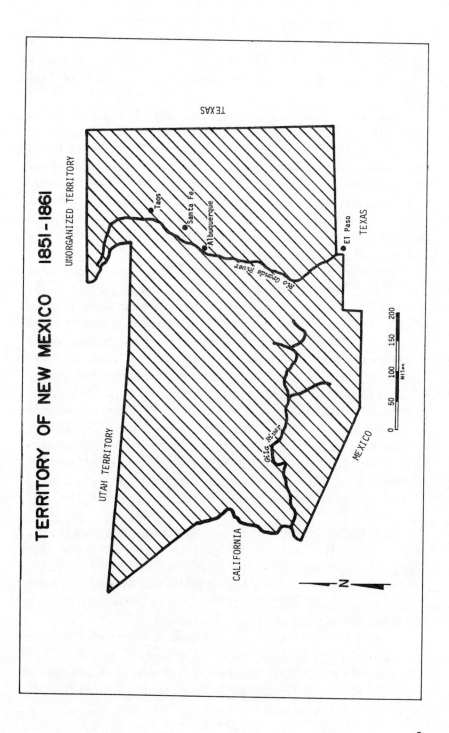

TERRITORY OF NEW MEXICO   1851-1861

UNORGANIZED TERRITORY

TEXAS

UTAH TERRITORY

CALIFORNIA

Taos

Santa Fe

Albuquerque

El Paso   TEXAS

Rio Grande River

Gila River

MEXICO

N

0   50   100   150   200
Miles

but according to the Rcd. opinion, as to the location, of the line I entered the Territory, on the twenty-second of August — although I did not reach the seat of government until the ninth of September."[1]

The Texas boundary dispute dated back to the year 1836, when, after gaining independence from Mexico, the Congress of the Republic of Texas declared that the boundary in the southwest and west was the center of the Rio Grande under the terms of the alleged Treaty of Velosio that ended the conflict. With this declaration, Santa Fe, the most heavily populated region east of the great river, was included in the domain of Texas. But the vast bulk of the Mexican population rejected this boundary decision as they had no desire to be ruled by Texans.

This determination not to be part of Texas was manifested in 1841 when a Texan army numbering three hundred men under the command of Hugh McLeod invaded New Mexico. Their purpose remains clouded in controversy. Many Mexican-Americans and the American merchants from Missouri in New Mexico maintained that seizure of the territory claimed by Texas in 1836 formed the real objective. On the other hand, the journalist George W. Kendall insisted the group was organized for purposes of trade. If this was indeed the case, their political intelligence was quite faulty, for instead of being welcomed as traders the Texans were considered to be invaders and were surrounded by Mexican-Americans commanded by Damaso Salazar who compelled them to surrender. Two of the party were shot and the rest packed off to Mexico where they were imprisoned until the summer of 1842 and then released.[2]

The Texans lost this round but did not abandon their dreams of expansion. Had not Andrew Jackson earlier suggested they claim not only New Mexico but California as well? As a result, even as the war between the United States and Mexico was being fought, plans were being formulated in Austin to pursue the claims of Texas to all territory east of the Rio Grande.[3]

Was the claim of Texas legal? Was it justified under the then international guide to adjudication of disputes, Emerich de Vattel's *Law of Nations?* Did the stated opinions of past and present political and military figures justify their claim? The answer to the

first of these questions is in the negative, for the basis for recourse
to the *Law of Nations* lay in the policies of Spain and Mexico in
their administration of the region, and both Spain and Mexico
considered New Mexico and Texas to be separate provinces.[4]

On the other hand, in answer to the second question, several
military and civil officers, including United States President Polk,
made official statements that provided the Texans with justification for their case. One of these individuals was the commanding
general of the Army of the West, Stephen Watts Kearny, who,
when he entered Las Vegas in 1846, issued a proclamation from
the roof of a building on the plaza in which he stated: "We consider it [the Territory of New Mexico] and have done so for some
time, as part of the territory of the United States."[5] Another was
Francis Preston Blair, recently appointed U.S. attorney general.
While searching for justification for bringing to trial on a charge of
treason the Mexicans who had participated in the abortive Taos
uprising against the Americans in 1847, Blair reasoned that these
men were citizens even though New Mexico was not part of the
United States by right of conquest. In his opinion, the territory had
always been a part of Texas which was in the Union.[6] Finally,
Polk himself stated on one occasion that he would never permit
a second power to occupy any territory east of the Rio Grande.
Certainly, therefore, by 1846 the Texans could assume that with
a United States victory in the Mexican War, federal recognition of
their claim was almost inevitable.

Secretary of the Treasury Robert J. Walker made a decision
on the eve of the war with Mexico in 1846 that pointed to a
contradiction in federal policy and resulted in embarrassment to
the administration. Walker's action, which occurred in the spring,
was the outgrowth of the practice of allowing a rebate of tariffs
collected on all imports to the United States that were scheduled
to be exported to Mexico, including Santa Fe, in their original
packages. When Polk stated that all territory east of the Rio
Grande was part of the United States, Walker ordered these payments of "drawbacks" to cease.

The Missouri merchants, who were the major carriers of these
goods from the United States, were outraged by this order. Immediately they appealed to the Congress, and the situation became

so tangled that Walker brought the matter before the cabinet. There it was decided to continue the payments of the reimbursements for the moment. Such was the air of uncertainty that characterized administration policy. However, the Whig press played havoc with the administration's decision and did not allow Polk to forget the matter easily.[7]

There was no uncertainty in Santa Fe, at least not among the articulate Hispanos capable of expressing their thoughts in the language of the conquerors. They joined in common cause with the Missouri traders, who feared the possibility of trade competition from the Texans, and with the army officers, desirous of retaining the positions of authority they had attained in the government recently organized by Kearny, in arranging protest rallies against transfer of the region to Texas, and made known their opposition in the press:

> We are disposed to laugh at the complacency with which the governor and the Legislative Committee of Texas, in solemn-council assembled, advanced the preposterous claim, but we regret to state that the *smile* is not the only thing excited by a perusal of this strange document. *Contempt and pity!* Contempt for the names who set up such a claim, and pity that so many fools could be found in a free and enlightened state to sanction it. . . . Upon what rights, real or fancied, does the Legislature of Texas enact the law of December 18th, (A.D., 1836 . . . ? Was it *conquest* or was it *purchase?* We have yet to learn that a Texan soldier ever trod the soil of New Mexico other than with his ears cut off, or as a prisoner of war; and as for purchase, the actual financial condition of Texas is sufficient evidence that such purchase was never made but thanks to our friends—the traitors have plenty of tar and feathers.[8]

In 1847 the Texas government was inclined to play a waiting game. For the moment they attempted to strengthen their position by granting head right donations east of the Rio Grande in the hope such a policy would drive Mexicans across the river thinking they would be in Mexican territory. By 1848, however, the governor and the legislature, outraged at the procrastination on the part of the federal government, passed legislation declaring Santa Fe and the area east of the Rio Grande a Texas county. They organized the Eleventh Judicial District, and appointed Spruce McCoy Baird to Santa Fe to assume judicial duties in the new district. The new judge thought he would experience little difficulty in organizing and administering his district. Soon after his arrival in Santa Fe, however, he was subjected to disillusionment when Colonel J. M. Washington, the military commander and acting governor of the new Territory of New Mexico, supported by the Missourians and Mexican-Americans, made life a torment for the aspiring judicial official. Meetings were called protesting his presence, proclamations were posted calling for him to leave, and his declarations of authority were ridiculed.[9] In the end, after months of fruitless effort and the failure of the Texas legislature to pay him, Baird resigned his position and turned to a mediocre political career in New Mexico.

The Texans were not through. In 1850, just as the controversial boundary question was reaching fever pitch in Congress, the Texas legislature divided the land claimed by Texas east of the Rio Grande into four counties. Robert S. Neighbors, who had been the federal Indian agent in El Paso, was appointed commissioner and assigned the task of organizing governments in the new counties. He had little trouble in completing the task in those counties lying wholly or partly in the territory that was undisputed. When he arrived in Santa Fe, however, he, like Baird, encountered some difficulty when Colonel John Munroe, the new commander of U.S. troops in New Mexico, issued a call for a meeting of a constitutional convention despite Neighbors's protestations that such an act was a violation of the Constitution and a denial of the Texas claims. Further, Neighbors insisted that such a call to meeting constituted creation of a state (New Mexico) within a state (Texas) and without the consent of that state. Munroe rejected the protestations of Neighbors and the separate-statehood movement in New Mexico continued, with all political factions in the territory, aside from a few opportunists, closing ranks against the intruder from Texas.[10] The determination was to resist to the death the "unjust usurpation of Texas."[11] One of the judges appointed by Kearny, Joab Houghton, insisted that he would imprison anyone seeking to enforce a law of Texas. He further stated that while every effort would be made to employ peaceful methods against the Texans, force would be utilized if necessary. The New Mexicans, said some, must be ready to employ military force.[12] The realization that his cause was hopeless without military assistance finally hit home in the mind of Neighbors, and he left Santa Fe. In the aftermath of his departure, the populace celebrated another victory over the hated *Tejanos*.

Meanwhile, as the above events were taking place in New Mexico, passions were mounting in Congress. The eyes of the nation were focused on the Texas boundary issue because of its relation to the question of slavery expansion. Many Northerners of an anti-slavery disposition believed that even if the conditions in the Southwest were not conducive to the development of a plantation system, slaves might yet be employed profitably in small-scale agricultural pursuits as well as industrial or mining activities. They believed that the expansion of slavery must be halted. Thus, arguments dealing not only with the questions of legality and constitutionality but also morality continued to mount in intensity in both houses of Congress from 1846 through 1850.

Senator Thomas Hart Benton, because of the economic interests of his home state of Missouri in New Mexico, was particularly concerned that the crisis there be resolved as soon as possible. As a result, he proposed in 1850 that the Texas boundary in the west follow a line along the 102nd meridian from the Rio Grande north to latitude 34 degrees, and then east to the Red River. The southern boundary of New Mexico would be the Rio Grande from the point of confluence with the Pecos, west to El Paso where it would proceed in a westerly direction.[13] (See map, The Texas Claim.)

The New Mexicans were delighted with this proposal, for it would extend their border east of the Llano Estacadeo (staked plain) in conformity with the traditional Mexican description of the boundary between the two former provinces of Texas and New Mexico. The Texans, however, were outraged, for now they stood to lose land *east* of the disputed territory. The only gain for Texas would be the region of El Paso with which the state had been geographically, economically, and historically connected.

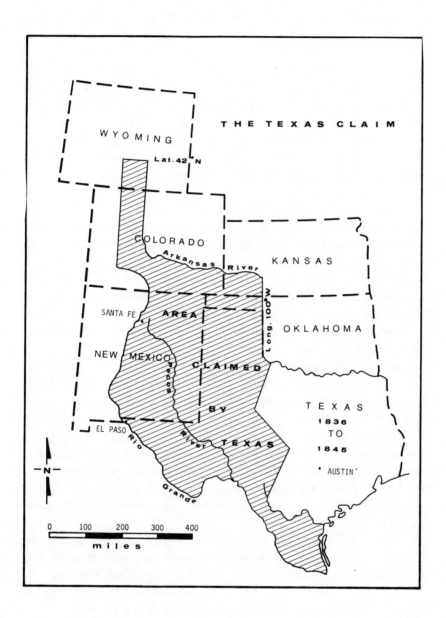

THE TEXAS CLAIM

11

A second plan was put forth by Senator Henry Foote who recommended that two states be formed from Texas and the disputed territory. The first, to be called the State of Jacinto, would include all of Texas east of the Brazos and the Rio Grande, with the land west of the great river divided into three new territories: New Mexico, Deseret, and California. Foote's proposal had its origins in the congressional resolution passed when Texas was admitted into the Union which stipulated that in the future as many as five states might be formed from the original cession. Moreover, the senator from Mississippi calculated that his plan would satisfy those who were opposed to Texas being of such great geographic size.[14]

Another attempt at appeasement was made by Senator John Bell of Tennessee. He proposed that three states be organized south of a line formed by the Red River and 34th parallel running west to the Rio Grande. One state would include territory east of the Trinity River, the second would lie between the Trinity and the Colorado, and the third would include land between the Colorado and the Rio Grande. Bell supported the Texans in their claim that the Rio Grande formed the southern and western boundaries of the United States.[15]

Finally, Henry Clay offered a proposal that a line be drawn from a spot twenty miles north of the Rio Grande to run obliquely in a northwesterly direction until it reached the point of intersection of the Red River with the 100th meridian. He reasoned that the territory which would be lost by the New Mexicans contained communities that preferred to be a part of Texas, while the area that would be gained by them would provide sufficient compensation for the loss. Clay also proposed that the Texans receive financial remuneration equaling their public debt before admission to the Union.[16]

The conflict was not restricted to New Mexico and Congress, for acerbic exchanges also took place within the press as reflected in the following editorial appearing in the *New York Tribune*:

> To hesitate or waiver as to the effrontery and baselessness of the claim as set up by Texas to push her boundaries and her jurisdiction up to N. lat. 42 degrees and bring Santa

Fe, Taos, Albuquerque, and nineteen-twentieths of the New
Mexicans under her abhorred dominion, is to presume most
grossly on the American people's ignorance. . . . *There is no
New Mexico if the Claim of Texas is valid* . . . she is a weed
and a ruin.[17] (Italics author's.)

This view best captured the truth of the situation, for whoever
controlled the heavily populated east side of the Rio Grande possessed the key to the Southwest. Thus, one can better appreciate the
adamant stand assumed by the anti-slavery *Tribune*.

It was Senator James A. Pearce of Maryland who introduced
the plan which was ultimately accepted. He proposed that the
western boundary of Texas start at the 36°30' parallel and run
southward along the 103rd meridian to the 32nd degree of north
latitude and along that parallel to the Rio Grande. Aside from the
northern line being shifted to the 38th parallel, and other relatively
minor changes, the last one taking place in 1891 to the advantage
of Texas, this arrangement brought about the final solution of the
New Mexican boundary problem in the east and was signed into
law by President Millard Fillmore on September 9, 1850. The
hatred that existed between Mexican-Americans and Texans, however, was further exacerbated by the boundary struggle and served
as a decisive factor in the Union successes in New Mexico during
the Civil War.

The Economic Life of New Mexico

2

Agriculture

Within the vast territory that was New Mexico, the Anglo-Americans who came in the mid-nineteenth century discovered two cultures clustered along the banks of the Rio Grande and its many tributaries: the Pueblo Indian and the Mexican-American. Living in villages of various sizes and running from the Rio Arriba region above Santa Fe to Socorro in the south, they formed a continuous line of civilization until a point of departure leading into the dreaded Jornada del Muerto was encountered. This area was a desert that extended eighty miles to the south before blending into a second fertile region along the Rio Grande in which were located Dona Ana and Las Cruces in New Mexico and El Paso in Texas. Surrounding the villages were barren plains and mountains inhabited by the hostile Indians of the Plains. Hence, a scarcity of water combined with the need for common defense forced the Mexican-Americans and Pueblos to cling to the river. As the culture of Egypt was the gift of the Nile, that of New Mexico was the gift of the Rio Grande. The cluster-like pattern of villages made for "cultural cohesiveness and permanence of influence."[1]

The centers of Mexican-American settlement were small in population; the only one numbering more than four thousand was

15

Santa Fe. Other of these settlements included Taos to the north, and Albuquerque and Belen to the southwest. Linking these larger towns together were numerous little villages. The Pueblo Indian villages in 1846 also varied in size. According to the merchant Charles Bent, the largest pueblo along the Rio Grande was located at San Felipe and contained over four hundred families. Other important villages were Santo Domingo, with three hundred families, and San Juan, containing over two hundred families; the remainder ranged in size from twenty families at Pojoaque to one hundred and twenty at Isleta.[2]

Although the economy boasted some craftsmen, it was basically pastoral. The lack of rainfall made it essential that the Pueblo Indians and the Mexican-Americans exercise strict control over the distribution of water. This fact necessitated the construction of waterworks, including reservoirs and acequias (irrigation canals).[3] Even the Hopis, who lived some two hundred miles northeast of Santa Fe, and practiced dry-farming techniques, maintained reservoirs in the crevices of the mountains. These were fed by the flow of water from springs above. As a result they were able to create islands of fertility within a sea of aridity. It is ironic to note that these people lived in an area contiguous to a strip of land on the San Juan River, measuring one mile in width and two hundred miles in length, that was extremely fertile. It was too dangerous to occupy, however, because it was accepted as a buffer zone separating the Navahos in the south from the Ute Indians to the north.[4]

The origins of the irrigation technology and system of management of the acequias can be traced to the processes employed by the peasants of southern Spain, who in turn were influenced by Moorish techniques, as well as the methods practiced by the Pueblo Indians.[5] It was, however, the early Spanish ordinances that defined the responsibility for the regulation and distribution of water. Moreover, the Spanish methods of acequia farming encouraged intensification of the use of canals among the Pueblo Indians who adopted several Spanish customs of management.[6]

For example, in the village or town, the mayordomo (ditch chief) was responsible for construction and management of the acequias as well as for distribution of water. In the pueblos, the duties were shared by two individuals: the ditch chief who supervised the erection and maintenance of the acequias, and the cacique who controlled the dispensation of the water on religious lands. As long as the rivers were high and water plentiful, little discipline was required. When the water level fell, however, a period of scarcity made it necessary for the mayordomos in the towns and the caciques in the pueblos to exercise their authority by insisting that permits be obtained from them before any water could be used in the fields or for household purposes.[7]

An acequia provided water for arable tracts that ranged in size from three hundred to three thousand acres. The first step in constructing the system was the digging of the *acequia madre* (mother ditch), or public canal. Massed forces of labor were necessary to accomplish this task which meant that the landowners had to provide a large number of peons who worked along with the small farmers in the performance of ditch-digging tasks.[8] In the pueblos all other duties were suspended at mid-morning when the ditch chief summoned the inhabitants to the point of construction.[9]

In order for the force of gravity to be employed, it was necessary that the river be tapped at a point above the lands scheduled to be irrigated. At that point the diggings were commenced on the *acequia madre* which was normally fourteen to fifteen feet in width, two to six feet in depth, and ran the course of the land to be irrigated. The one at Santo Domingo was seven and one-third miles long.

After work was completed on the main ditch, the workers next turned their attention to the construction of the *contra acequias* (secondary ditches), or, as they were referred to in the pueblos, *sangrias*. These, and still smaller ones, led from the *acequia madre* to the fields being irrigated. Floodgates were erected at each opening in order to control the water flow, with acequias being built on both sides of the river.[10]

Once the acequias were constructed they had to be maintained in operational condition. Annual repairs were necessitated by the erosion from the swift flow of water and by the sudden overflows that sometimes ruptured the banks. When the acequias ran dry, as was often the case in late July or August, each landowner was required to provide one hand for fifteen to twenty days of labor. Much of the work consisted in repairing the floodgates and widening and deepening the channel, with most of the emergency repairs made in the spring. All hands reported to the ditches when the alarm bell in the church pealed, for this was the warning of a freshet and subsequent break in the floodgates.[11]

In the Rio Abajo (the land down the river below La Bajada) the system was employed in the most efficient fashion. By 1850 this region was so highly cultivated as to be considered the most productive section of the territory.[12]

The problem of managing the acequias remained one of the most pressing responsibilities of all echelons of government as the continued existence of life was completely dependent on their efficient operation; and the need for massed labor to construct and maintain the acequias resulted in a social-political organization that was oppressive in nature. The continual dependency on irrigation remained a source of anxiety until the coming of the railroad and the development of dry-farming techniques.

In the realm of politics, the governors were constantly besieged by individuals with grievances resulting from what they felt to be violations of their water rights. This circumstance held true in the Spanish, Mexican, and American periods of control, for the people felt they must go to the highest authority with a matter of such grave concern. No one could tolerate the building of any structure which would interfere with the flow of water. One of the first concerns of Governor James S. Calhoun after organization of the Territory was that "a just system of irrigation is demanded," and he gave statutes dealing with water regulation a high priority.[13] Letters, official records, and newspapers tell of petitioners seeking redress for damages done to their fields, or for relief from potential destruction of their landholdings. In 1827, for example, the Mexican governor, Manuel Armijo, had to intervene personally to force a landowner to remove the logs he had placed in his acequias so that the waters would rise and feed his sangrias to the disadvantage of another occupant downstream.[14] Even the most powerful autocrat of Taos, Father Antonio Jose Martinez, whose power went almost unchallenged prior to the coming of the Americans, found himself faced with an armed rebellion when he attempted to dig an acequia that, while benefiting him, would have threatened the water supply of the Indians of the pueblo.[15]

D. V. Whiting, in his position as territorial Secretary of the Treasury, was constantly faced with complaints, such as the following in 1851:

> Received petition of Serafin Ramierez in name of twenty persons of Alameda complaining or protesting against a decision of the Prefect of Bernalillo County, respecting an Acequia; accompanying said petition was an order from the late Judge Otero and opinion of Attorney General: petition transferred to Mr. Ashurst [Attorney General].[16]

In 1852, as an example of the quarrels over water rights between the two tribes, the Navahos claimed that the Laguna Indians had robbed them of their rightful water and complained to the acting Superintendent for Indian Affairs, John Greiner, who noted:

> This question of right to water, is one of the most difficult to settle that we meet with, especially with the Pueblos. For instance take this one case and it is one of many. The Navahoes owned a fine piece of land and they had sowed it with wheat. The grain was growing finely and they looked forward to gather a plentiful harvest. The Laguna Indians claim the grain above them as theirs, and in irrigating their fields they cut off the water from the Navahoes, whose crop is at once destroyed. This case has been referred to Gen'l Baird, the Agent to investigate and to decide.[17]

As late as 1870 it was reported that the "small supply of water in the creeks from which the irrigation acequias are supplied made for a rivalry between the planters to obtain the use of the water."[18]

The governors attempted to relieve themselves of these pressures by authorizing the county prefects and justices of the peace and, later on, the probate judges, to resolve the problems dealing with the acequias. Often, however, the petitioners refused to be satisfied with the decisions of these lesser officials and continued to carry their appeals to the governors. Recourse was also made to the legislature, as when Governor Calhoun called for laws designed to establish regulation of the water supply.[19] Some procedure was needed if disputes involving rico landowners, independent, Mexican-American farmers of small property, Pueblo Indians, and the members of the Navaho nation were to be resolved.

Fear of a drought and famine was always present in the minds of these people as their geographic isolation made them completely dependent on their crops. In 1860 Governor Abraham Rencher expressed the universal dread when he wrote that the corn crop was a "partial failure" because of the drought. Moreover, the year was one of "great scarcity" and provisions were expensive.[20] One year later he stated, "At time some suffering because of the partial failure of last year's crop. Much concern over the long, cold, dry spring. Makes people fear for the coming growing season."[21]

This was a different land from the fertile fields of Iowa and Missouri, and, as the *Missouri Republican* noted, "Our farmers would cut a sorry figure squatted in little valleys and depending on irrigation. Some say more land can be tilled—however, all that can be irrigated [is] now being tilled."[22] It was only after the threat from the Indians had been removed that the Anglo-Americans were able to develop the dry-farming techniques and artesian well projects that enabled them to find a place for themselves in the agricultural environment of New Mexico. In the meantime, they sat back and viewed contemptuously the Mexican-American struggle for survival.

Anglos continued to move into New Mexico, attracted by its economic possibilities, especially in agriculture. They were, however, appalled by the backwardness of the agricultural techniques employed there. One observer described these methods:

> No branch of industry in New Mexico has been more neglected than that of agriculture, which seems to be in about the same condition as when the Spaniards first settled the country. It has been pursued merely as a means of living, and no effort has been made to add science to culture in the introduction of an improved mode of husbandry.[23]

Overlooked by the Anglo observers was the fact that it was only as a result of the skill developed in managing the acequias that the Mexican-Americans had survived to employ their crude methods of subsistence farming. Instead, the Anglos were inclined to concentrate on the primitive nature of agricultural management. Particularly were they annoyed over the fact that only eight hundred square miles of land, all that could be irrigated, was being cultivated. Many were convinced that the American talent for invention could devise the means of making more water available for irrigation.[24]

The implements used to farm the land were also objects of derision. It was claimed that they were the "same . . . that Cain used six thousand years ago."[25] For example, the plow consisted of nothing more than the crotch or knee of a tree. One branch served as the body of the plow; the other, the handle. More often it might be made from two sticks of timber with the body being beveled at the tapered point and shod with a piece of sharp iron. Also there was mortised into its upper surface, about midway, a *tranca* (pole) which played vertically through the plow-beam. The beam, resembling a wagon tongue, was fastened to the plow at the junction of the handle with the body, and raised or lowered on the *tranca*. A team of oxen was attached to the beam with two men tending each plow, one to guide the machine, the other to goad the oxen. As many as fifteen plows might be observed working a single large field.

The fields were irregular and the rows were so crooked as to call forth the derision of the Anglos. Sickles were used to cut the staple crops of wheat and corn, the former being cut and gathered when it was very dry. The grain, however, adhered to the sheath and did not shatter on impact. After being hauled from the fields, the grain would then be threshed by cattle on earth floors. The corn was cut early in order to use the leaves and stalks as fodder, and to safeguard it against frost and thieves. A *fanega* (approximately 2.25 bushels) on some occasions brought as much as ten dollars in Santa Fe. Other grain crops such as rye, barley, or oats, were not raised.

Other crops grown in New Mexico included beans, peas, onions, lentils, beets, radishes, cabbages, pumpkins, and chili peppers. Tobacco (*punche*) was also produced along with fruits which included apples, pears, peaches, and grapes. Anglos were amazed by the size of the beets and the good quality of the cabbages and radishes. They mourned the fact that tomatoes did not grow well because of the cool climate, and potatoes were rare. A continuing source of dismay to the Anglos was the fact that the lands were not enclosed.[26]

As is universally the case with farming, the harvests varied from one year to the next. In 1851, for example, despite drought, hail, and grasshoppers, the yield was quite good and so were the prices. Corn brought $4.00 a fanega in the Rio Abajo and $6.00 to $7.00 in Santa Fe. The correspondent who relayed this news suggested in a burst of enthusiasm that such prices would encourage "a sizeable migration to New Mexico." He went on to suggest that the irrigated lands were better than those in Missouri and Illinois since they produced from forty to sixty bushels of wheat an acre. Becoming more optimistic, he suggested, "We can find more mines of gold tilling the soil rather than performing the tasks of infinite toil as they do in California."[27]

Although this man obviously exaggerated the agricultural potential in New Mexico, he was perceptive enough to appreciate the possibilities for the development of new lands not yet tenured. There were years of crop shortages, however. One occurred in 1846 when a near famine resulted from the abnormal demands made on the food market by Kearny's Army of the West. By August, corn, when available, was commanding a price of $3.50 a bushel.[28] As a result, both farmer and consumer suffered during the following winter.

Governor Abraham Rencher gave official expression to the Anglo hope for success in agricultural pursuits when he stated in his 1857 message to the legislature that, while the territory lacked "fructifying showers," there were acres that might be planted if suitable grains and modern implements were employed. He also suggested that the federal government subsidize experiments with Chinese sugar.[29]

An editorial the same year in the *Santa Fe Weekly Gazette* proclaimed the Anglo hopes for the future:

> We have stated on a former occasion that nothing is so well calculated to produce the general impulse desired as agricultural associations or Farmers Clubs.... Let the large land and sheep owners there come together and form associations,

one for each county, or a general association representing the whole district. Through such associations every farmer who desires it could be put in the way of access to agricultural books and journals containing the information he stands in need of. Once familiarized to intercourse of this kind, the members would freely interchange ideas and discuss with intelligence and interest the pursuits they are engaged in. Little by little, a healthy emulation would manifest itself, and as consequences, farms would improve, better modes of culture would be introduced, choice breeds of stock would make their appearance more frequently, and the face of every farming district would be so beautified that the fathers of the present generation, if they could rise from the dead and gaze again on the sites of their slovenly fields, would not know the land they once inhabited.[30]

All that was necessary for "progress" was for the Mexican-American to follow the lead of the Anglo and the road to prosperity was assured. As a consequence, many soldiers mustered out of service, traders possessed of money after the sale of their goods, and others traveling to California were attracted to the possibilities of agricultural life in New Mexico.[31] The way was paved for eventual Anglo-American dominance of the land in New Mexico.

But the Mexican-Americans refused to become commercial farmers despite Anglo pressures—at least not in the nineteenth century. They continued to conform to subsistence-farming techniques. In 1883 the *New Mexican Review* complained that cultural backwardness was due to the failure of the Mexican-Americans to compete with outsiders.[32] They were content to satisfy their own needs with just a bit left over for a few "luxuries."

In a sense, therefore, the backwardness of the Mexican-American farmers' agricultural system, combined with the attempts of Anglo-Americans to convince them to adopt their techniques and values, represented a contest between "barbarism and civilization." The Anglo-Americans felt these "alien and inferior people" must conform to the Anglo concept of progressive development in agriculture as well as other activities if they were to be successfully incorporated into the "American system" and not remain foreigners. Consequently, perhaps such "backwardness" provided "justification" for Anglo-Americans to embark in the land expropriations that followed in the late nineteenth and twentieth centuries.

Mining*

In a letter to Secretary of State James Buchanan, Governor Charles Bent suggested a need for "laws for the regulation of mining . . . this being the principal and almost only source of wealth and education."[33] This interest in mining, of course, dated back to the moment when the first Spaniard entered the territory, intent on discovering his El Dorado. Consequently, thousands of mining ventures took place, many of which escaped the attention of historians. The Anglos were extremely interested in mining possibilities in New Mexico, and paid close heed to the stories of mining enterprises of the past and suggestions of possibilities for the future. They naturally compared Mexican-American techniques with those with which they were familiar. Josiah Gregg was a particularly interested observer. He noted that gold mines were the richest ones in New Mexico and that the most important mine was located at the Real de Dolores, also known as the El Placer, about twenty-seven miles south of Santa Fe. Gregg estimated that over $500,000 in gold was removed from this mine between 1828 and 1844. And more gold was present to be mined if the "want of energy and enterprise" that characterized the native population was replaced by Anglo ambition, for only a small portion of the gold region had been mined. Moreover, the ore averaged about $19.70 to the ounce troy at the Philadelphia mint, which meant that the traders would pay as much as $17.30 per ounce troy of gold at Santa Fe.[34]

The crudity of mining techniques employed by the Mexican-Americans disgusted the Anglos. A hole was dug in the earth and a ladder consisting simply of a pole with notches cut in it was placed diagonally in the hole. The miner descended the ladder, dug a sack of earth and returned with it to the surface where he

*This essay first appeared in *El Palacio,* the magazine of the Museum of New Mexico, P.O. Box 2087, Santa Fe, N.M., and is reprinted with the permission of the editors.

then turned the bag of dirt over to the washers, in most instances his wife and children. They would then fill a round bowl called the batea with the earth and immerse it in water as they stirred it with their hands, until all of the dirt floated off leaving but a few grains of gold in the bottom. No windlasses were employed, nor was any type of machinery known to those people. And, as Gregg scornfully noted, any attempts to introduce machinery were rejected by the Mexican-Americans who feared, quite accurately, that the Anglos had designs on their mines.[35]

The scarcity of water forced the miners to do most of their work in the winter because of the availability of snow that could be passed through a tube placed between heated stones, resulting in water flowing into the pan. No mention is made by Gregg or other Anglo-American observers of the pain suffered by those forced to stir the nearly frozen water with naked hands.

The laws governing the operation of mines allowed an individual a wide freedom of action. Any person could dig a mine as long as it was at least ten paces from the ones already being worked. The end result was a type of communal arrangement that further repelled the Anglos. In fact, the only instance of a large mining enterprise before the coming of the Anglos was the Ortiz Mine in the Dolores area. It dated back to 1833 when the commanding officer of the Mexican garrison protecting the region, Lieutenant Don Jose Francisco Ortiz, was granted some 1,550 linear feet of land for mining purposes. He in turn permitted other miners to jointly occupy the property as he profited from the goods and food they purchased at his store. Like the other mines in the region, this one continued to be productive, and when Ortiz died in 1848 he left the property to his widow.[36]

The economic opportunities that were so obviously present in the Ortiz Mine could not help but attract those Anglos on the entrepreneurial make. One of them, John Greiner, secretary of the territory, managed in 1853 to form a syndicate that included a group of political cronies in Ohio, for the purpose of purchasing the Ortiz Mine. After purchase, N. P. Miller, who had gained recognition as an engineer, was placed in charge of the mine and, although he lacked modern equipment, began operation in 1854. By 1858 it was obvious that, while gold was present, without equipment the production would never be enough to provide adequate profits.[37] Therefore, Greiner and his associates decided the time had come to incorporate the operation in an effort to raise sufficient funds to purchase the needed machinery. To incorporate, however, it was necessary to obtain a charter from the territorial legislature and the approval of Governor Abraham Rencher. Soon it became obvious that this end could be accomplished only by a distribution of shares among the more influential members of the legislature and other prominent territorial officials. Not until near the end of the year was a charter obtained from the legislature. Abraham Rencher, Henry Connelly (who succeeded Rencher as governor), Manuel Otero (the territorial delegate), and other prominent New Mexicans were listed as stockholders. By the middle of 1859 all of the shares were sold and the company was "regularly organized."[38]

Once equipment was acquired, production increased to the point where sizeable profits were being realized by 1860. Consequently, the promoters decided to secure further the property by having Congress confirm the grant. With little difficulty Otero managed to achieve this objective in 1861. The owners thus ensured themselves permanent possession of the property despite the fact that in the original grant made to Ortiz, permanent possession of surface rights was prohibited. Although mining operations were interrupted by the Confederate invasion of 1862, they were resumed after the war with the greatest profit being realized in 1868.[39]

Anglo interest in mining activities was not restricted to the Ortiz grant. The decade of the fifties witnessed an extraordinary number of miners penetrating into New Mexico and southern Colorado searching for the strike that continued to elude the vast majority. Letters appearing in the press spurred the search.[40] One correspondent, writing from Santa Fe, insisted that "the mineral resources of Mexico [New Mexico] are only surpassed by the hospitality of her citizens."[41] A second miner spoke of finding gold pieces, one "weighing fifty ounces."[42] Senator Thomas Benton, after receiving a report that the Ortiz placers were producing $250,000 worth of gold in 1849, urged Congress to pass the organizational act that would provide the security which Anglos demanded before they would move into the territory to share in the wealth.[43]

Interest in the Gila River country to the south was aroused in 1851 when a miner told of taking in an ounce of gold each day. This report was further substantiated in 1852 when a "Mr. Chastide," a veteran of the California rush, suggested that the Gila deposits were richer than those in California. The enthusiasm engendered by such reports inspired a party of forty veterans, traders, and other fortune seekers to undertake the hazardous fifteen-day journey to the rugged Gila River region.[44] Those who returned to Santa Fe some weeks later told of encounters with Indians and a failure to find gold; most of the "Gila Boys" finally decided to strike out for California.[45] Other miners sought gold in the region between Mora and Las Vegas and in the Taos country where it was reported that a Pueblo Indian was murdered by the Indians of Taos for telling the Anglos of the possibility that a gold mine was located in the region.[46]

Silver mining was attempted by some individuals. In 1852 Serafin Ramierez hired twenty hands to work in a lead mine at Arroyo Stando, eight miles from Santa Fe, because he hoped it contained silver. One month later a second rico, Don Antonio Sandoval, invested $8,000 in the venture and thereby became a partner. By May 3, Ramierez and Sandoval had mined and smelted two pounds of silver to be assayed in Philadelphia. The success of this venture encouraged further silver mining activities in the region.

The largest silver deposits were found in the southern part of the territory. In the Sierra de los Organos near La Cruces, two mines were discovered, and as a result, hundreds of emigrants heading for California changed their minds and either sought employment in the mines or attempted to make their own strikes. The correspondent for the *Missouri Republican* noted with satisfaction that the large growth of the Anglo population now meant that the Mexican-American laborers in the mines could be dismissed.[47]

One of the mines had been discovered by an individual known simply as "Old Louis." He sold three-quarters of his holdings to Esler Hendree, district attorney for El Paso County in Texas, in order to protect himself against "exploitation." Shortly afterwards the old man sold his remaining quarter to the rico brothers, Mariano and Pedro Ogogie. By the end of July the mine was producing one dollar's worth of silver for every five pounds of ore. These mines excited national attention. Even after the yield was reduced to eight dollars' worth of silver to every three hundred pounds of ore, the lead included in the deposit added to the profit.[48] Copper mines had also been discovered in the same area, and Anglos, fresh from the states, were engaged in at least four separate copper mining activities by 1854.[49]

By the late fifties and early sixties these numerous mining enterprises led to a feeling of economic optimism.[50] The mines in the south were doing well; topographical parties surveying the Pacific Railroad route were seeking the locations of new mines, and Kit Carson, noting the rush of miners from Pike's Peak to the San Juan Basin, suggested that the mines in that area of New Mexico were "richer than California."[51] Governor Abraham Rencher, asking Congress to provide funds for a geological survey, boasted that mineral wealth was present in all areas. He suggested the possibility that the territory might be found to be the richest one in the United States if Congress would appropriate but $25,000.[52] W. W. H. Davis predicted, "When the mineral wealth of New Mexico shall have become known, I have no doubt the capitalists of the United States will turn their attention this way, and enter largely into mining." The only reason a rush had not yet occurred, according to Davis, was due to the fact that the "common occurrence" of wealth was not universally known.[53]

Sheep Industry*

In 1851 the New Mexico reporter for the *Missouri Republican* complained in a dispatch to his readers, "Were you to witness ... our life you could appreciate the sincerity of my words. We have mutton, and mutton, and mutton, and mutton three or four different kinds of meat, as you see."[54] Mutton was plentiful because

---

*This essay first appeared in *El Palacio,* the magazine of the Museum of New Mexico, and is reprinted with the permission of the editors.

the most flourishing industry in New Mexico by the beginning of
the decade of the fifties was sheep raising. It always was an important activity as Josiah Gregg attested in his classic *Commerce
of the Prairies*:

> Nothing, perhaps, has been more systematically attended to in
> New Mexico than the raising of *sheep*. When the territory was
> at the zenith of its prosperity, *ranches* were to be met with
> upon the borders of every stream, and in the vicinity of every
> mountain where water was to be had. Even upon the arid and
> desert plains, and many miles away from brook or pond, im-
> mense flocks were driven out to pasture; and only taken to
> water once in two or three days. . . . Sheep may be reckoned
> the staple production of New Mexico and the principal article
> of exportation. Between ten and twenty years ago, about two
> hundred thousand head were annually driven to the southern
> markets; indeed, it is asserted, that, during the most flourish-
> ing times, as many as five hundred thousand were exported in
> one year. This trade has constituted a profitable business to
> some of the *ricos* of the country.[55]

The Anglos who came after the Mexican War were naturally
attracted to this lucrative occupation which promised to be even
more profitable with the elimination of tariffs and the opening of
new markets in California. The number of sheep in New Mexico
doubled between the years 1846 and 1861.

The Mexican-Americans, however, continued to maintain a
stronghold on the industry because it provided the average peon
with his best opportunity for social mobility. Juan Augustin de
Escudero, an observer of conditions in New Mexico, described the
process a poor Mexican-American went through in his rise from
"rags to riches": The shepherd would appear before a rico and

> . . . offer to help him take care of one or more herds of
> sheep. These flocks were composed of a *thousand* ewes and
> *ten* breeding rams, which were never separated from the herd
> as is the practice of stockholders in other countries. Conse-
> quently, in each flock, not a single day would go by without
> the birth of two or three lambs, which the shepherd would

put with the ewe and force the female to suckle without the difficulties which he would have had with a large number of offspring. The shepherd would give the owner ten or twenty per cent of these sheep and an equal amount of wool, as a sort of interest, thus preserving the capital intact.

From the moment he received the flock, the shepherd entered into a contract in regard to the future increase, even with his overseer. As a matter of fact, he usually contracted it at the current market price, two reales per head, the future increase to be delivered in small numbers over a period of time. With this sum, which the shepherd had in advance, he could construct a house, and take in other persons to help him care for and shear the sheep which was done with a knife instead of shears. The milk and sometimes the wool from the said sheep provided him with subsistence; the wool was spun by his own family into blankets, stockings, etc., which could also be marketed, providing an income. Thus the wealth of the shepherd would increase until the day he became, like his overseer, the owner of a herd. He in turn would let out his herd to others after the manner in which he obtained his first sheep and made his fortune. Consequently, even in the home of the poorest New Mexicans [shepherds], there is never a dearth of sufficient means to satisfy the necessities of life and even to afford the comfort and luxuries of the wealthiest class in the country.[56]

With prices increasing from $.50 a head in 1831 to $2.50 in 1851, the sheep industry continued to grow despite the attacks of Indians and subsequent losses of vast numbers of sheep.[57] In 1851 one Anglo reported owning a flock ranging from two thousand to twenty-five hundred head. He appointed a mayordomo to take charge of the herd and hired two fourteen-year-old boys to assist him. Dogs were trained to aid in controlling the sheep, pastured in an area ranging from one hundred and fifty to two hundred miles in extent. The salary paid the mayordomo was not reported, but the boys earned from three to four dollars a month, plus one-half fanega of corn monthly and the right to kill a sufficient number of sheep to keep them in meat. This Anglo owner valued the carcasses and not the wool, although the sheep were shorn each spring to "keep them in health." He predicted that his flock would increase to about four thousand by the end of 1852 and fifty-five hundred head by the end of 1853. Consequently he hoped to increase his investment of $3,000 to over $9,000 with $1,300 being deducted for expenses. He then planned to invest his profits in mules, as the price for one had increased from $20 to $80 or $100.[58] Some owners had as many as fifty thousand sheep in their flocks and were realizing enormous profits in the decade preceding the Civil War by driving the sheep to California.[59] Among the more famous drives were the ones conducted by Kit Carson, who in one instance drove six thousand and fifty head across the old Spanish trail to Los Angeles, and those conducted by "Uncle Dick" Wooten who in 1852 moved nine thousand head to the Pacific Coast.

The largest drive took place in 1854. Trader Francis X. Aubrey joined forces with Judge A. J. Otero, Francisco Perea, and Jose Francisco Chavez to drive over forty thousand head of sheep across the desert to California. The profits were fantastic as they received six dollars a head in return on a $1.50 investment.[60] Both the owners and the fifty-five herdsmen were well satisfied despite the perils of the trip (on one occasion they discovered the bodies of ten men who had been killed by the Indians).[61] Aubrey never reaped any of the benefits from his newly acquired wealth as immediately upon his return to Santa Fe he became engaged in a quarrel with Richard Weightman and was killed before he had "taken off his specia."[62]

Manuel Alvarez, always attracted to the possibility of profit, also entered the sheep business. He came close to experiencing a financial loss in 1852, however, when Don Damas Lopez, to whom he had entrusted over four thousand sheep to be driven to California, died after successfully crossing the Colorado River. A new administrator was appointed who continued the drive to San Diego where the sheep were put up for sale. But in a letter from W. Z. Angney in November, Alvarez was informed that the whole thing was a "bad business"; the Mexican-Americans were offering to sell the sheep at five to six dollars a head when a better price could be commanded.[63] In January Angney wrote again: "I fear your business has fallen into bad hands. They were sold at a sacrifice price. Had Lopez lived on and the affair been managed well you would have realized handsome gains. We sold out at 8.25, your sheep—

some 3300 were disposed of at 6.25, and ought to have brought more."[64]

So concerned was Alvarez on receipt of this letter that he invested Francis X. Aubrey, who was preparing to conduct his drive to the coast, with the power of attorney in order to ensure that the money received for the sheep would be in trustworthy hands for delivery to him. Aubrey reported that the situation was not quite as bad as Angney depicted it: the administrator had collected $26,633.12. Aubrey estimated that after paying off the shepherds and other claims, including a five-percent fee to the auctioneer, he would have over $20,000 for Alvarez, who finally received his money but only after many months of anxiety.[65]

The next year, 1854, saw the price of sheep fall to $5.00 a head, even in San Francisco, as a result of an excessive number being driven to the coast from New Mexico.[66] This sum still represented a sizeable profit, however, and flocks continued to be driven to California during the fifties. One observer, S. A. Hubbell, reported that over 105,000 sheep were shipped to the West Coast in 1858. So great was the demand that upon arriving at Pajarito, New Mexico, a group of herders constructed a ferry (at a cost of $2,500) which they carried to the Colorado River to transport the sheep across the stream.[67] The industry flourished to the point where a group of Anglo sheep owners were willing to pay up to $300 a head for a number of French Merinos purchased for breeding purposes.[68]

The possibilities of reaping additional profits from the manufacture of woolen textiles was not lost on the eager Anglos. As early as 1847 the *Santa Fe Republican* discussed the possibility of capitalizing on the abundance of sheep and erecting woolen mills:

> The vast sums of money annually expended in the purchase of woolen goods in the United States and Mexico, in cloths, blankets, etc., would be retained in the territory and would probably enhance the general prosperity. Instead of sending out a large amount of money to buy woolens, it would be dispersed over the territory and could be made itself a source of profit by application to some other branch of business. How extensively manufactures might be prosecuted, and

whether a market other than that at home is attainable, are questions not now to be settled. They will arise one day, and it may, in anticipation, be asked, why may not the luxuries of St. Louis be bought by the Nigro cloths of New Mexico? Why may not the great cheapness of wool enable us not only to compete with, but undersell the eastern fabrics? And why may not woolen goods form a good backloading to wagons returning from the east?[69]

Ten years later Abraham Rencher in a message to the legislature decried the fact that while the territory was rich in pasturage the surplus wool was allowed to rot away or else was shipped to the States for manufacture. This was "nonsense," he stated, for it would not require much capital to construct the factories that would allow New Mexicans to purchase woolens at from one-fifth to one-fourth the price then being paid.[70]

Support for a textile factory continued to mount until 1861 when two acts established the San Miguel Manufacturing Company and the New Mexico Wool Manufacturing Company. Unfortunately, as was the case with so many other enterprises, the Civil War intervened to bring a halt to the construction of these mills.

Mexican-Americans were still controlling the sheep industry at the outbreak of the war in 1861. The Anglos, however, had gained control of a sufficient amount of land to provide them in the years following the conflict with the wedge that enabled them to become as powerful a force in ranching as they were in mining and agricultural activities.

PART II
THE PEOPLE OF
NEW MEXICO

The Mexican-Americans— The Insiders Looking Out

The Cultural Background

The Mexican-American is the product of three cultures—Spanish, Mexican, and Indian. Unfortunately, this obvious truth has been either ignored or rejected by Hispanos (many Mexican-Americans in New Mexico preferred to be referred to as Hispanos or Spanish-Americans) who sometimes cling to the Spanish tradition as a means of achieving the degree of prestige and status enabling them to be accepted by the Anglo-Americans as equals. This behavior has resulted in the Spanish tradition being overemphasized while the Mexican and Indian have been submerged.

Fortunately, younger Chicanos today realize these facts and are willing to accept the term Mexican-American[1] for they recognize and take pride in the composite make-up of the people of New Mexico. Take, for example, the Church Census of 1790 in which one discovers the following population distinctions (paraphrased from the Spanish):

INDIAN OF THE PUEBLO. One who has maintained his identity as a Pueblo Indian and has not intermarried.
COYOTE (COLLOTE). One who is part Indian and part Spanish.
SPANISH. One who has not intermarried and subsequently maintained his Spanish identity.

GENIZARO. An individual whose origin was unknown and generally considered to be from one of the tribes of the plains.
MESTIZO. One who has in his lifetime arrived from Mexico.
MULATTO. One who is the product of marriage between a black and Spaniard or of a mixed strain including all of the above.
HOMBRE DE COLOR (man of color). A shade lighter than the Mulatto and several generations removed from the marriage of a black and one of the above.

The most startling entry in the Census, however, reads: "Vecenie Rodriquez, *Native of China*" (author's italics).[2] This individual must have arrived in New Mexico from China by way of the Philippines and through Mazatlan or one of the other ports on the west coast. What is interesting, is that as a result of his marriage to a Spaniard, children were born who were officially referred to as *Spanish*.

Such processes of intermingling continued until by the middle of the nineteenth century the practice of making such sharp distinctions ceased. Although there were those who paraded forth their blue eyes as proof of pure Hispano heritage, the masses were products of the intermingling of Indian and Spanish bloodlines. As a result, by the time of the American conquest, a subtle passage from Coyote or Genizaro to Mexican-American had been completed in scores of thousands of cases.

The Census of 1850 shows that the population, exclusive of Indians, amounted to 56,984. Of this number not more than 550 were of Anglo extraction. The vast majority, therefore, were Mexican-American in population composition.[3] The socio-economic and political framework within which they were enclosed was more feudal than capitalistic; that is, it resembled more the plantation economy of the South than the industrial and small-farm economy of the East and Midwest.

The Peonage System

The economic base for this form of existence was the peonage system. Peonage resulted in generations of families being subjected to enforced servitude as the result of some ancestor contracting a debt. Under the law the courts could not intervene to prevent mistreatment unless the peon complained; and they were so illiterate as to be unaware of their right to assume the judicial initiative.

Two forms of peonage existed: voluntary servitude wherein the peon became indebted and worked for a paltry recompense of from two to fifteen dollars a month, which invariably resulted in a life of bondage as expenses always exceeded income; and involuntary servitude derived from the practice of capturing and holding by force Indian slaves taken in wars. It is the first type that will be examined at this time while discussion of the latter form will take place later in the chapter.

There is no greater proof of the import attached to the system of peonage by the ricos and Anglo-Americans than the instructions given the delegate to Congress by the Convention of Delegates in 1849 when it was stated he should: "have inserted in said constitution [for the territory] a provision which shall secure the compliance with contracts between masters and servants according to the interests of the parties."[4]

And included in Governor James S. Calhoun's first message to the legislature in 1851 was this recognition: "The relations between masters and peons should be distinctly defined, and each should understand their respective obligations and appropriate remedies for the violation of them upon the part of either, should be provided."[5] The "interests" of which the delegates spoke were those of the ricos; and the "obligations" that Calhoun stressed were those of the peons.

The Anglo-Americans in Congress were inclined to view with a great deal of interest the institution of peonage. Some were inclined to contrast it with black slavery so as to prove under Mexican laws the illegality of black slavery in New Mexico. Congressman Richard Donnell was one of these as he insisted that peonage, based as it was on debt, was different from black slavery inasmuch as there was the possibility that the debt might be paid and the enforced servitude come to an end. Thus, he reasoned that the Mexican law allowing peonage did not legalize slavery and that the one outlawing black slavery was just as valid as any in the United States which prohibited black servitude.[6]

Most observers, however, considered the peons to be worse off than slaves. During the Mexican War Senator John M. Clayton noted that the peons "are in a worse condition of slavery than our negroes, and would be happy to change places with them."[7] Representative George Marsh insisted that laws should be passed in consideration of that "barbaric relic of the ancient Roman law, peonage."[8]

As far as the masters were concerned, peonage possessed several advantages over slavery; it was enforced servitude without the master having to make the original investment incidental to buying a slave. Moreover, the master was not subject to taxes or to the losses suffered by slaveholders upon the death of slaves. In addition, the ricos had little to fear from the right of the peon to free himself through repayment of his debt, for seldom, if ever, was he able to pay it. As one observer noted, the black man could just as easily buy his freedom. Finally, the master was not responsible to care for the peon in his old age as he was simply "cast adrift to provide for himself."[9]

The laws regulating peonage under both the Mexican and American governments were slanted in favor of the master. Wages were unbelievably low, as already noted, averaging about five dollars a month. Women were paid even less, and while some masters threw in amounts of chili and beans in addition to the money, conditions of extreme poverty were only too common. In addition, the peon was forced to buy all of his goods at the master's store, where, despite laws to the contrary, he had to pay the exorbitant prices that further perpetuated his condition of indebtedness. Thus the same dismal pattern was repeated: the peon not only spent his life in a state of complete servitude but was forced through continued and increased indebtedness to bind out his children.

The man who represented the interests of the master was the mayordomo who acted as overseer. He usually earned from twenty-five to fifty dollars a month.[10]

It is difficult to capture the instances of human suffering and hardship inherent in such an institution, but occasionally a bit of evidence comes to light. On one occasion, an attractive girl of sixteen was placed in servitude as a peon, having been sold by her father to pay a debt he had contracted. She appealed to General

James Shields, the military commander in the area, who promptly paid the debt when he discovered it was but five dollars, and ordered the girl returned to her family after beating off her attempts to kiss his feet in thanks.[11]

The Anglo-American governors, all Southerners, cooperated with the ricos in retaining the institution of peonage. On May 10, 1851, Calhoun heard the complaint of a Tesuque resident that another resident had taken a child belonging to him. After examining witnesses, the governor decided in favor of the plaintiff and had the child returned to him as a piece of chattel property.[12]

In another instance Calhoun insisted that while children must remain with parents, the prefects would enforce the jurisdiction designed to protect the interests of the master to whom the family belonged.[13] Other Anglos, in return for political favors, either practiced benign neglect or gave active support to the peonage system. In fact, some, such as the merchant-governor W. A. Connelly, actually owned peons.[14]

Not until after the outbreak of the Civil War were any firm measures to end involuntary servitude attempted. In 1861, despite the combined opposition of Connelly, General James Carleton, and Congressional Delegate Francisco Chaves, William F. Arny, who was appointed Territorial Secretary, mounted a vigorous campaign to eliminate peonage. Supporters of continuance of the system insisted that it was too deeply impressed on Mexican culture to be dismissed; that to do so would harm all parties concerned, the master who could not farm his land without peons, and the peons who could not care for themselves.[15] Consequently, it was not until 1867 that the persistent abolitionists Charles Sumner and Henry Wilson, senators from Massachusetts, were able to push through Congress legislation designed to complete the job of the eradication of all forms of indentured servitude in the United States. Wilson was in a particularly advantageous position to enforce the new law as he was chairman of the Military Affairs Committee and could thus put pressure on the army to execute the statutes. Under this legislation, peonage was abolished and those who violated this restriction could be fined from $1,000 to $5,000 and imprisoned from one to five years. Civil and military officials were made responsible for enforcing the law, and Wilson threatened court martial for officers who were derelict in the performance of their duties. By 1870 the system had largely disappeared, although some charges of enforced servitude were made as late as the close of the nineteenth century.

The peonage system was a degrading feudal hangover that was preserved in New Mexico because of ignorance on the part of the masses, indifference on the part of the Anglos, and selfishness on the part of favored Hispanos. It was allowed to continue as an institution for another twenty to thirty years after the occupation by the Anglos, because of their willingness to overlook the evils present in this situation of indentured servitude in return for favors and political support from the more powerful native families.

Mexican-American Reaction to the Anglo Occupation

Following months of tension, Congress declared war on Mexico on May 13, 1846. Two days later, Colonel Stephen Watts Kearny was organizing the Army of the West, and on June 3 he was ordered by William L. Marcy, Secretary of War, to invade and occupy New Mexico and California. The initial reaction of New Mexicans to news of the invasion was universal fear of the intentions of the invaders. Mexican-Americans drove their stock into the mountains, secured their possessions, and put "themselves in a position to be out of harm's way at a moment's warning."[16]

But in the aftermath of Mexican Governor Manuel Armijo's abortive attempt to defeat Kearny, the city of Santa Fe assumed a festive air, at least on the surface. One observer reported:

> On the arrival of General Kearney [sic] and his troops, they proceeded to make a dazzling exhibition of their ceremonies, so as to impress them with an idea of the pompous character of the church. . . . About eight o'clock at night the town was brilliantly illuminated by the pine fagots that blazed from all the walls of the city, from the tops of the churches and the private houses. For four hours, there was a continual discharge of fire-arms, throwing of skyrockets, and fire balls. The elements were red with long streams of fire for three hundred feet high. The rockets would sometimes explode in

the air, and again fall among the crowd and explode, causing great confusion. While this was going on, in another part of the square there were some fifteen hundred persons, mostly women, sitting on the ground, listening to a comedy, or some kind of theatrical exhibition. Everything said was of course in the Spanish language. Next day the celebration was renewed. The church was crowded to overflowing, though ample enough to contain two thousand persons. Six priests officiated at the altar, which was lighted up with twenty-four candles. General Kearney [sic] and staff officers, and some of the officers of the volunteer regiment were present. During the whole time, singing, instrumental music and the firing of musketry, were strangely commingled. Towards evening horse racing, dancing, and gambling occupied the attention of the throng.[17]

This feeling of approval was further intensified by Kearny's proclamation that he planned to protect the people from the Indians who had plagued them over such an extended period of time. More than one Anglo felt certain that the people were pleased with the change in government.[18]

But immediately in the aftermath of the occupation, an air of uncertainty was apparent as the people simply did not comprehend the new system of law that was being forced on them. "It is my bad luck to have been appointed Sheriff," stated Fernando Aragon, newly appointed jefe of Taos, in a letter to acting Governor Donaciano Vigil in 1847, "because I do not understand these laws. Please teach me to understand this new code."[19] Vigil, a respected Hispano, had been appointed as acting governor after Charles Bent was assassinated in Taos in 1847. While Vigil continued to serve as governor through 1848, he was subordinate to the American commander Sterling Price.

In another instance a prominent justice of the peace, Desidero Baca, resigned his position when his decision in a case was subjected to judicial review and reversed. The loss of face that he experienced made it impossible for him to continue in the position. He had to conform "to the dictates of an independent mind" and could not allow his office to be made a "laughing stock."[20]

In the period of confusion following the establishment of Kearny's government, many Mexicans were purposely misled by Anglos into retaining their Mexican citizenship as a means of reducing the number of Mexican-Americans possessed of the franchise. As a result, these people had no civil rights and might be compared to the metics of Athens who were also dispossessed of their rights. In many instances those who were disenfranchised never obtained the right to vote.[21]

But the most revealing incident displaying the lack of a common ground of understanding between the Mexican-Americans and the Anglos developed over the matter of the military chapel. In Spanish and Mexican times this was a place of worship for the troops. After the occupation, however, it was employed to store arms and was seized as United States property. In 1851 when the American commander, Colonel E. V. Sumner, removed the stores, Judge Grafton Baker received permission to use the chapel as a courtroom. When news spread that the building was going to be renovated, despite the fact that it had been abandoned for twenty years, a crowd immediately gathered before the place of worship and vigorously protested the desecration of their sacred edifice. Tearful women kneeled and kissed the floor of the holy place, and when the grand jury was summoned, many refused to take the oath in the converted courtroom. Judge Baker called on the local commandant, Colonel Edwin Brooks, for help. But, that officer was aware of the hostile mood of the population and returned the chapel to the first American bishop appointed after the conquest, Jean Baptiste Lamy, much to the prelate's surprise. It is probable that this act alone prevented a riot from taking place.[22]

The evidence provided by the reactions of the Mexican-Americans to the ways of the Anglo-Americans illustrates that there was a need for a period of adjustment; as one octogenarian in Taos expressed the feeling of his people several years ago: "If they had but given us twenty years to learn their customs before forcing them on us we would have been better prepared to protect ourselves."[23] However, charged the Mexican-Americans, the Anglos insisted on immediate conformity to their code. The result, according to present-day descendants, was economic loss, political subjugation, and social dismemberment, as the following evidence gathered in a survey of 350 Mexican-American students in northeastern New Mexico in the fall of 1971 indicates. (I realize this method entails a broad jump in time. However, I believe the collective oral history technique is valid among a people so dedicated to preserving an oral history tradition.)

The first question put to the students was designed to determine what percentage of students were descendants of Mexican-Americans living in New Mexico during the period under study. It reads as follows:

Were any members of your family living in New Mexico in the years 1840 to 1865?

The answers were:

YES	79.4%
No	5.3%
NOT SURE	15.3%
NO ANSWER	———

Of those who responded in the affirmative, 39.7 percent said stories of conflicts between Anglos and their families had been passed down from generation to generation; 22.1 percent said they had not been; and 38.2 percent were not sure. Of those telling the stories 2.3 percent were fathers; mothers comprised 0.8 percent; 13.4 percent were grandfathers; 11.0 percent grandmothers; 2.4 percent great-grandparents; 7.9 percent came from other relatives; and 62.2 percent were not sure.

According to the students, 1.5 percent of the storytellers told tales favorable to the Anglo-Americans; 9.9 percent were ambivalent; 61.6 percent were decidedly unfavorable; and 27 percent were uncertain. Of the students who testified, 18.5 percent said their families suffered a decrease in landholdings, while 7.7 percent cited instances of decreased political power, and 16.2 percent claimed a loss of social prestige. The remainder were not certain of the nature of the losses suffered by their ancestors.

Only 1.6 percent of the storytellers said they had always witnessed conditions of equality, while 15.6 percent *usually* expe-

rienced equal treatment. Thirty percent noted occasional conditions
of equality; 28.1 percent said seldom were they treated as equals;
and 16.4 percent charged that they had never been accorded equality of opportunity in any category of activity. The remaining 4.7
percent expressed no opinion.

Moreover, the 93.7 percent who felt there had been instances
of inequality suggested the following reasons:

Land seizure by Anglos 3.3%
Anglos felt superior 5.0%
Anglos discriminated against Mexican-Americans
    socially and economically 6.6%
Language and cultural differences taken advantage of 6.6%
Land seizure by Anglos, and Anglos felt superior ... 1.7%
Land seizure by Anglos, and Anglos discriminated
    socially and economically 0.8%
Land seizure and language and cultural differences
    taken advantage of 0.8%
Anglos felt superior and Anglos discriminated against
    language and cultural differences 3.3%
Anglos discriminated against Mexican-Americans
    socially and economically, and language and
    cultural differences 1.7%
Anglos exploited Mexican-Americans 9.1%
All of the above 58.7%

But the ancestors were most emphatic when asked by the
students how often they were subjected to conditions of inequality,
as the following responses indicate:

ALWAYS 28.0%
USUALLY 35.2%
SOMETIMES 28.0%
SELDOM 5.6%
NEVER 2.4%
DON'T KNOW .... 0.8%[24]

The suspicions present in the minds of the Mexican-Ameri-

cans on the eve of the Anglo-American conquest and in the aftermath of the occupation were carried over to later generations. The
storytellers thought the Mexican-Americans suffered some form of
economic, social, and political inequality at the hands of the Anglo-
Americans, and passed these beliefs down to their descendants.

The Indians

4

The Indians of the Pueblos

"We chased them [the Pueblos] to the river [the Rio Grande]; there we allowed them to remain for it suited our purpose to trade with them and raid their gardens for food each year."[1]

Although this is a boast out of machismo, there is some degree of historical accuracy to the statement. The Pueblos did settle along the great river and its tributaries; but except for the revolt against the Spanish at the close of the seventeenth century and the abortive Taos uprising in 1847, they remained peaceful despite raids each year by the Indians of the Plains. Not that some Anglo-Americans did not fear the possibility of a Pueblo uprising. James Calhoun charged that his political enemies in 1851 were inciting a rebellion among them in their attempts to "rule or ruin." Troops were dispatched to Taos, considered to be the trouble spot, but no uprising took place.[2]

According to Charles Bent, who was well informed because of his business relations with the Pueblos, the Pueblo villages contained the following numbers of families at the time of the American occupation in 1846:

Taos—200 families	Santa Clara—20 families
Picures—80 families	Santo Domingo—300 families
Abequi—40 families	San Felipe—400 families
Nambe—50 families	Caciuteo—60 families
San Juan—200 families	Sandilles [Sundice]—
Pojoaque—20 families	160 families
Tesuque—60 families	Isleta—120 families
San Ildefonso—40 families	Acoma—100 families
Jemez—no figure	Laguna—200 families
Zuni—100 families	Sodente—200 families

Santa Anna—no figure[3]

In addition, there were the Hopi Pueblos of the San Juan Valley that included some two hundred and fifty families. The pueblo at Pecos had fallen into ruins, not only because of Indian raids, but also as a result of the encroachment by Mexicans on the land of these Indians. After they were reduced in number to but four families, the Pecos Pueblos moved to Jamez in the west. Altogether there were probably no more than twenty thousand Pueblo Indians left out of forty thousand when the Spanish came in the sixteenth century. Their villages stretched from Taos in the north to Isleta in the south.

One of the most prosperous pueblos in the territory was Taos, despite having lost some acequia rights and grazing lands to Mexican-Americans and Anglos, according to John Greiner, the Indian agent. The inhabitants appeared "happy," their pueblo had a school, and "nearly all of them know their letters."[4] Such was not the case with the Picares on the southeast side of the Taos Mountains. It was a favorite raiding ground for the Jicarilla Apaches and by 1850 the pueblo was in a "ruinous condition."[5] San Juan was thriving as the acequias were in good condition and the lands were under cultivation while the population was increasing and the cacique was planning a school for the children.[6]

Santa Clara, thirty miles north of Santa Fe, had lands too high to be irrigated from the Rio Grande. Consequently, they depended on a small creek that flowed into the river from the mountains as a source of water for their *acequia madre*. Some Mexican-Americans attempted to erect a settlement above the village and construct acequias which would have rendered all Pueblo land worthless. Unable to produce a title, however, they were forced to abandon the project.[7]

San Ildefonso, located on the east bank of the Rio Grande, had a fine plaza but presented a unique problem inasmuch as half of the houses were occupied by Mexicans. As a result, the population was divided and constantly quarreling one with the other to the point that Pueblos were leaving the village.[8] Pojoaque, located on the creek of the same name, had also been inundated by Mexican-Americans. It was the smallest and poorest pueblo in the territory and was doomed to extinction. On the other hand, Nambe, three miles to the east, was in good condition; the same story held true for Tesuque.[9] The pueblo of Zuni, numbering more than five hundred people and located two hundred miles west of Santa Fe, was constantly subjected to various annoyances from the Navahos and Anglo emigrants en route to California, who stole sheep, mules, horses, and grain by posing as purchasing agents for the government.[10]

Three common dialects were spoken by the Pueblos, none of which was understood by the vast majority of Mexican-Americans. These tongues included the Tesuque spoken by the Cochiti, Santo Domingo, San Felipe, Santa Anna, Acoma, and Laguna Pueblos; the Quiquas dialect spoken by the Taos, Picuris, Sandia, and Isleta Pueblos; the Pecos language spoken by the Pecos and the Ierney Pueblos. It is interesting to note that the Taos and Picuris Indians in the north spoke the same language as the Isleta and Sandia Pueblos in the south, and that the Pecos in the east spoke the same tongue as the Jemez in the west. All of these Pueblo Indians, however, were able to understand one another.[11]

The Hopis spoke a fourth form of Pueblo that was not easily understood by the other Pueblos. Living two hundred miles to the northwest, they inhabited eight villages near the San Juan Valley, and raised little else but corn in their fields. Wearing blankets and leggings, the Hopis appeared more like the Indians of the Plains than Indians of a pueblo. When a group visited Santa Fe in 1851, there existed a language barrier when the Anglos wished to address the Hopis, which was only resolved by each question being put to a Mexican interpreter; he then translated it into Spanish to a Santo Domingo Indian, who next put it in his dialect to a Dominguese woman who had intermarried with a Hopi; she then translated the question into the language of the Hopi being addressed.[12]

Soon after the occupation the Americans became aware that the Pueblos provided a unique problem, for they were unlike any of the nomadic Indians heretofore encountered; rather, they were a civilized people permanently located in their villages. Such a situation prompted Governor Calhoun to note in his first message to the legislature in 1851:

> There is not a more difficult problem, arising in this Territory than that of a proper disposition of our Pueblo friends. What should we do with them? They are here, in our midst, surrounded by our New Mexican population, and rightfully, in my opinion, without authority to mingle in our political affairs. These people, however, must necessarily have the same protection that is afforded to the most favored. It is a well known fact, that they own portions of the richest valley lands in this Territory, and why should they be exempt from paying a just proportion of the taxes which must be raised to support the Territorial Government? Concede this point and another question, necessarily arises. They are tax paying residents, but not aliens, and are you prepared to elevate them to full fellowship? I cannot recommend such a union. But it is inevitable, they must be slaves (dependents), equals, or an early removal to a better location for them and our own people, must occur. This subject is one of vast import, and should be well considered, and, if you agree with me, Congress should be memorialized in relation to the position which you may be pleased to assign to them. It is perhaps advisable, to pass an act, authorizing the extension of the laws of this Territory, to such period as may be necessary to consult the Government of the United States, in reference to the policy to be pursued, with these Indians. That policy should not be disturbed. In the meantime, however, I, recommend that if any one, or more of the Pueblos, should manifest a desire to abandon their separate existence, as a people, that the laws of the Territory be immediately extended over them, under such regulations as you may prescribe.[13]

No attempt was made to assimilate them and they were not

granted citizenship, although actions were taken to protect their rights. In 1850, in his capacity as superintendent of Indian Affairs, Calhoun noted:

> I have been incessantly annoyed by complaining representations, made to me, by deputations from the Pueblos of Santa Anna, San Juan, Tesuque, and Pojoaque. The two first complaining of encroachments upon their lands, by Mexicans —The first has been brought into the Circuit Court of the Territory, to defend their claims to lands, which they say they have always possessed, and which was formally and legally granted to them.[14]

No sooner were the Pueblo claims in this case upheld than Calhoun was faced with another dispute in which he wrote:

> One of the Indians of Tesuque was sued in the Alcalde's Court of this place, by a man, who says he left a mule in March last with the Indian alluded to; that he did not apply for the mule before last August, and as he did not get a mule, he sued the Indian in December last. Obtained judgement, execution issued and on the same day he returned "Satisfied." And yet, on the 6th of this month, the plaintiff goes to said Pueblo, about eight miles from this place, with another individual, with this "Satisfied" execution, and not being able to find the latter defendant, he seizes one of his mules, and has him now in his possession, *as his own property.* I have notified him, the present possessor of the mule, that if he did not restore him, I would send his conduct before a Grand Jury. And this I may do; but what will it avail? For with the *ignorant* Indians of this territory, (Neither of the three Judges even studied law for a moment, I presume until they were appointed Judges by General Kearney, [sic] in 1846) *justice* is just blind enough to favor the strong at the expense of the weak; and consequently I may fail in my attempts to protect the Indians, and with them, must necessarily lose *caste,* and their confidence in the *justice and power* of the Government of the United States is, in the same proportion, diminished.[15]

One fascinating case that caught Calhoun's attention involved a black man who allegedly drove off two cows belonging to the Pojoaque Indians. He was brought before the alcalde in Santa Fe and charged with theft but was acquitted. The Indians next turned to the district court where they sued the black man for the value of the cows and obtained judgment against him. Before the money could be collected, however, he was off for the "States." No mention is made of how he came to be in New Mexico or if he was heard of again after the incident. Calhoun simply stated he was going to take steps to ensure that the Pojoaques in the future would be protected from "negroes."[16]

The Pueblos on occasion brought charges against the Church. Particularly were they concerned over the fees imposed on them for the performance of clerical duties by the priests. Calhoun, not wanting to become engaged in a church-state conflict, cautiously told the Pueblos to act "according to custom."[17]

The most persistent complaint, however, was that the Mexican-Americans were encroaching on the Pueblo lands.[18] In 1852 John Greiner, who was acting as Superintendent of Indian Affairs following Calhoun's departure, complained: "The Pueblos are planting their grounds and digging their acequias. If they could be protected from the depredations of the Mexicans they would be excellent examples to light as well as red brethern."[19]

Even Calhoun was not immune to Pueblo charges of encroachment. In the summer of 1851 the Pueblos insisted that the governor and his rico accomplices intended to strip them of "their fine valley lands."[20] These charges were fostered by Calhoun's political opponents in an attempt to unseat him and were proven to be baseless. Thus, with the local Anglos and ricos exercising political power, the Pueblos became a political football subject to the whims and caprices of the territorial politicians. The problem was resolved with the abrogation of the post-Kearny legislation that gave the local politicos such control. Subsequently the federal government assumed full responsibility for the administration of Indian affairs.[21]

Neither were the Pueblos at peace with themselves. Quarrels were constantly taking place between the various villages. In one instance the Indians of San Juan complained that one of their number had been murdered by the Pueblos of Jerez. They appealed for justice in conformity with tradition, to Governor Rencher as their *tata* (father). By this time, however, the superintendency of Indian affairs had been divorced from the governorship so that Rencher had to refer them to J. A. Collins who occupied the Indian office. The Pueblos, now completely confused by the ways of the developing bureaucracy, gave up in disgust. The records do not show if they ever obtained the justice they were seeking.[22]

In the summer of 1851 rumors were rife that the Pueblos planned to revolt. As Calhoun told it, A. W. Reynolds, the defeated candidate for Delegate to Congress, and his party had spread false rumors that the lands of the Pueblos were soon to be seized. After forwarding a report to Secretary of State Daniel Webster, Calhoun urged the dispatch of troops to Taos and other points of danger in order to ensure that a repeat of the 1847 rebellion would not occur.[23] Two weeks of tension followed with the troops exercising vigilance and seeking to discover the leaders of the projected rebellion, while the Reynolds group continued to stir up discontent by exploiting a passage in a speech made by Calhoun wherein he stated that as wards of the government, they, the Pueblos, would not be elevated to "full fellowship."[24]

Calm prevailed, but in the aftermath of the incident, Calhoun determined to take the steps designed to ensure that violence would not take place among the Pueblos. Among these measures was the decision to have five Pueblos accompany him to Washington when he departed in 1852 to visit the capital and his home. Although he was critically ill when he left New Mexico, Calhoun still insisted that the Pueblos join the party as they prepared to cross the plains. He died en route but his secretary, D. V. Whiting, wired Commissioner of Indian Affairs Lea from Independence that the Pueblos were with him and requested funds to continue the journey for, as he stated:

> Governor Calhoun deemed it of utmost importance that a delegation of Pueblo Indians should visit the States at this time, not only for the purpose of carrying out the policy of the Government towards them, but also to secure more firmly their confidence and esteem towards our people. Evil disposed Mexicans and others have been tampering with them and en-

deavouring to induce them to join in a scheme for the purpose of overthrowing the present government. If these Indians are turned back, the consequences will be injurious to the Government and the territory alike.[25]

They continued their journey to Washington and four of them —Jose Maria, Carlos Vigil, Juan Antonio, and Jose Abeyta—all of Tesuque, after visiting the Indian Bureau, met with President Millard Fillmore in the East Room of the White House where they aired their grievances. Their complaints included the high price of food that left so little for clothing; the suffering they endured due to the raids of the Indian thieves; the stealing of water from the Pueblos by Mexicans through the illegal construction of acequias; and finally, the shortage of agricultural implements and church ornaments. Fillmore listened sympathetically and said that, while there was little he could do about the misbehavior of the Mexicans, he would request the newly appointed governor, William Carr Lane, to investigate the Pueblos' complaints, and he, Fillmore, would continue to look after their interests as he regarded the Pueblos as his children.[26]

The visit was fruitful. During the decade of the fifties, while they were able to obtain a total of but $15,000 in government doles, the Pueblos did succeed in having Congress approve their land claims before the Civil War, which is the most important reason for their survival as a people to this day.[27] Moreover, they achieved citizenship while retaining their tribal governments. During the Civil War, Lincoln sent each village chief a silver-headed cane as a symbol of authority.

The Anglos were much more inclined to accept the Pueblos than the Mexican-Americans; in Governor Rencher's opinion, the Pueblos were superior in manufacturing and agriculture "to the coarse Mexican population."[28] As a journalist noted in 1851: "*These* are good Indians. The only hope of civilizing the Red Man rests with them. We must leave them in peace and under our protection. . . . Build schools for them and we may soon make a comparatively civilized people."[29] Their amenable disposition combined with the fact that they willingly placed themselves under Anglo guidance and protection against the "recalcitrant" Mexican-

Americans serves to explain the popularity of the Pueblos among Anglo-Americans.

The Indians of the Plains

Whereas the government spent but $15,000 on the relatively docile Pueblos in its effort to preserve the peace, it was forced to expend over $30,000,000 in campaigns against the Indians of the Plains between the years 1850 and 1865. In this section the concern will be with common cultural traits of the various tribes who surrounded the cluster of Mexican-American towns and Indian pueblos along the Rio Grande.

Inhabiting the Cordilleras Mountains and adjacent plains, two hundred miles west of Santa Fe, were the Navaho Indians. According to Charles Bent, they numbered about ten thousand and occupied three hundred lodges.[30] Living in rude jacales (hogans) that somewhat resembled the wigwams of the Pawnees, they were divided into two groups by the Anglo-Americans—"The rovers and the sedentary ones."[31]

The rovers, the young tribesmen, were the troublemakers who made war on the Mexican-Americans and Anglos. The ones who were domesticated rejected fighting in favor of the development of skills, including the weaving of cotton textiles and production of the famous serape. This protective garment was so closely woven that it could be used as a water container and was in such demand as to command a price in excess of sixty dollars. Possessing great herds of horses, mules, cattle, sheep, and goats, the Navahos, according to Gregg, were superior to the Mexican-Americans in breeding animals. Their gardens, as well as their handsome buckskin clothing, also drew the admiration of Anglo-Americans.[32]

To the north were the Utes who formed a close alliance with the Jicarilla Apaches as a result of intermarriage. They were superb horsemen but possessed few skills that were not of a warlike nature. They numbered, according to Bent, some five hundred lodges and could mobilize over five hundred warriors in the wars in which they became engaged.[33]

The Apaches roamed the greater area and were divided into three tribal groups: the Mescaleros, east of the Rio Grande; the

Jicarillas to the north of the Mescaleros; and the Coyoteros to the west. These Indians raised no sheep, cultivated no land, and hunted little. Consequently, they lived off the produce of the Pueblos and Mexican-Americans and were notorious for raids in which they stole sheep, cattle and mules in great numbers.[34] Although no figure is available on the population of the Coyoteros, according to Bent, they were the most numerous; the Jicarillas numbered sixty lodges and the Mescaleros three hundred.[35]

One of the traditional practices of the Jicarillas, as related by a contemporary tribesman, was the ritual accompanying the return from the annual buffalo hunt. The medicine man had checkpoints leading from the hunting grounds in Kansas to the foothills of the Rockies. They sang as they sighted each peak forming a checkpoint. In all they made a total of four hundred and twelve stops before arriving at their goal at the base of the "Hill of Heaven"— Pike's Peak.[36]

In every tribe the lodges were wholly independent of each other in times of peace, as each one was administered by a head who was elected on the basis of personal popularity or kinship. The power of the family was tied in with the popularity of the head man and grew or diminished in conformity with his prestige. Families were united with others by a common language and association. Only in times of war, however, did the lodges present the appearance of a united tribe or nation when they elected a government consisting of the heads of families (petty chiefs) from whom one of great worth would be selected as the head chief. This one had to be able to rally all of the tribesmen around him. Consequently, both Indian agents and military personnel had to be careful in arranging a treaty to insure that the "chief" with whom one was negotiating really spoke for the tribe. In too many instances treaties were arranged with heads of families under the impression that the agreement was being signed with the tribal chief.[37]

The Anglo-Americans were particularly disturbed by the tendency of the Plains Indians to make war. In their opinion, the Indians of areas which had been settled earlier, such as the Old Northwest, had just cause for complaint against the white men who seized their land. But they did not feel that the Plains Indians had any justification for warring in New Mexico where vast areas continued to be occupied by the Indians of the Plains, and where Anglos, Mexican-Americans and Pueblo Indians occupied but small sections of the territory.[38] Forgotten, however, is the fact that the Plains Indians were dependent upon these settlements for their food supply, making it necessary for them to conduct raids leading to warfare.

The Indian Slave Trade in New Mexico

In New Mexico the question of Indian slavery far outweighed in importance that of black servitude. For while not as many as three-score blacks were to be found in the territory by 1860, present were well over three thousand Indians held in an informal and illegal state of servitude. The number *increased* during the Civil War as a result of the removal of the Navaho nation to the concentration camp at the Bosque Redondo in eastern New Mexico, as many of the Navahos who made the march were either forced to become slaves, or voluntarily accepted servitude rather than endure the sufferings of the Bosque.

The story of slavery in New Mexico dates back to the early days of Spanish settlement when the first ricos found themselves badly in need of workers, not only to construct and maintain the acequias and till the fields, but also to serve as shepherds for the numerous flocks of sheep. They quickly discovered a ready source of such labor in the docile children and women that might be taken from the roving tribes. In 1812 the Spanish governor complained that the Ute Indians were better armed than the Spanish as a consequence of their selling numerous captives to the settlers for fifty to one hundred dollars each.[39]

The most notorious of the Indian slave traders was the Utah chieftain, Walkara. He dominated the market at mid-century but by the middle of the decade was beginning to lose his grip on the situation. There were two reasons for this occurrence: first, the New Mexicans, in their desire to eliminate the middle man, began conducting their own slave raids; and secondly, the Mormons in Utah were opposed to slavery and took extreme means to prosecute any violations of the laws they enacted against the practice. Walkara died in 1859, and following his death the slave activities in Utah waned.[40] The practice, however, continued to flourish in New Mexico, for as Calhoun reported in 1850: "Trading in captives has been so long tolerated in this territory that it has ceased to be regarded as wrong; and purchasers are not prepared to release captives without an adequate ransom."[41]

Also, the slave trade was a two-way street, for in retaliation for Mexican-Americans capturing and/or purchasing Indian slaves from the Indians, the Indians captured and sold Mexican and Mexican-American captives to other Indians or Mexican-Americans. In 1845 the Apaches moved to within one mile of Chihuahua and not only killed several Mexicans but ran off with captives and three hundred mules.[42] James Russell Bartlett, the commissioner in charge of the Mexican border survey, tells how he was offered in return for the loan of rifles and ammunition, "a live Apache boy and girl too, if I wished; but having no desire for such additions to our party, I was compelled to decline the glorious proposal."[43]

In another instance a Mexican boy called Lopez was captured and hauled off into captivity by the Comanches. Although a reward of $2,000 was offered for his recovery, there is no mention that he was returned.[44] Sometimes the captives were sold in the same areas in which they were seized. Following one such instance, William S. Messervy, the secretary of the Territory, wrote a letter to Don Jose Maria Chavez, Judge of the Probate Court in Rio Arriba, in which he described how Juan Felipe Salazar of Abiqui had charged that Don Tomas Cabeze de Baca demanded that he, Salazar, surrender to him a fourteen-year-old boy that he had purchased from the Utes. The judge was advised that it was illegal for any "white person" to be held as property; therefore, Baca had no claim to the boy, and hence, he was returned to his parents.[45]

Another incident in which an individual claimed to have been sold into illegal captivity caused Messervy to issue the following proclamation:

> Whereas Jesus Arambulo y Solera has filed in this Office a Petition, to the effect, that one Jesus Lucero purchased him of the Indians in the month of April last and under said purchase claims him "as his Slave" and that the said Lucero, having shipped and otherwise maltreated him in the month of

August last he left the said Lucero and went to live in Manzana where he now resides that a few days since the said
Lucero went to Manzana and claimed him of the Alcade. He
now appeals to the Executive of this Territory of New Mexico
—call upon all the civil officers of the Government of this
Territory to give aid and protection to the said Arambulo,
that he may not be deprived of his liberty, in any way, form
or manner except by regular process of Law for Offences
committed against the law of the land or in such other cases
as may be provided by law.[46]

Few were so fortunate, for as Judge Kirby Benedict noted,
the captives who were entitled to their freedom did not know
enough to seek the aid of the courts to obtain their release from
bondage. He further observed that persons who held such captives
in servitude were extremely concerned about the money they had
invested in their human property, and were always inclined to dis-
courage recourse to the courts which would threaten what they
considered to be their property rights.[47]

In 1852 fifteen Navahos appeared in Santa Fe with three
Mexicans that they had captured and now held as slaves, and
turned them over to the authorities in the hope of receiving payment. When they failed to obtain any reward, they were bitterly
disappointed and suggested rather ominously that they would take
measures in the future to ensure the receipt of funds for any
slaves.[48] About the same time, a Captain Sailman arrived in Santa
Fe from San Antonio and reported meeting forty Comanches who
had just returned from a raid in their favorite territory in northern
Mexico, and had with them over six hundred horses and several
children they had captured near Durango.[49]

In many instances the Indians received commodity goods for
their captives. For example, on one occasion a ten-year-old Mexican boy captured by the Comanches in Mexico was sold to a Mexican-American family for the following merchandise: four knives,
two fanegas of corn, one plug of tobacco, four blankets, and six
yards of red cloth. Another boy of the same age, captured by the
Apaches, brought one mare, one rifle, one shirt, one pair of draw-
ers, thirty small packages of powder, some bullets, and one buffalo.

Finally, a young woman, whose husband and four-year-old daughter had been killed by Indians, was sold by the Apaches for two striped blankets, ten yards of blue cotton drilling, ten yards of calico, ten yards of cotton shirting, two handkerchiefs, four plugs of tobacco, one bag of corn, and one knife.[50]

The Mexican-Americans gave the Indians merchandise or animals for captives, but in selling them, received money from other Mexican-Americans. Paiute girls brought from $150 to $400, and boys from $100 to $300. In some instances the traders were known to go as far as lower California in their search for captives.[51]

One of the most serious charges made against Calhoun was that he had licensed slave traders to travel to the Salt Lake country for the purpose of buying and selling Ute children. In all probability the charges stemmed from the activities of one Pedro Leon who had gained recognition as the most notorious of the slave traders. He traveled to Utah in 1851-52 and made contact with the Paiutes who promptly stole eighteen of his horses. After he protested, they gave him nine children in return, four girls and five boys. Upon his departure the Indians complained to the Mormon alcalde, who then arrested Leon, fined him $50, and had him imprisoned for two months. After Leon appealed this decision to Calhoun, the rumor spread that the governor had licensed the trader to conduct his activities. The charge was false, but Calhoun knew of the slave trading and did little to stop the practice, because he knew that "the Mexicans had always engaged in extensive slave trade with the Indians and the common assumption was that the Indian children would lead a better life."[52]

In 1851 a New Mexican statute was passed regulating the division of all property captured in the continuing wars against the Plains Indians. It encouraged participation in the conflicts by those Mexican-Americans who wished to obtain slaves, as it stipulated that all captured property, including captives, would be divided among the members of the expedition upon reaching the settlements. Each was entitled to an equal portion and heirs of those killed were to receive first consideration. Officers who cheated were subject to court martial, but if they performed their duties, each was entitled to a double share.[53]

J. R. Bartlett, commissioner in charge of the Mexican border survey, suggested in 1852 that the Indians "must be annihilated or removed whence they can do no harm." Thus, he recommended that any expedition sent to fight the Indians should kill all warriors, but turn the women, children, "and such men as fall into our hands" over to the Mexicans.[54]

Those who owned Mexican-American or Indian slaves were disturbed by the fact that the institution was not formally recognized. In 1860 they tried to correct this situation by passing a bill that would have made the statute protecting Negro slaves applicable to other slaves as an act of "humanitarianism." Governor Rencher vetoed the legislation on the basis that, while the legislature had power to regulate slavery where it already existed, it could not create or abolish the institution. The Indians had never been slaves under Mexican or American law and therefore could not legally be made slaves. Then Rencher completely reversed himself for all practical purposes when he stated, "We can [however] hold them as captives or peons, . . ." a position that satisfied the ricos and Anglos for the moment. This act constituted another example of the Anglo and rico working together at the expense of the masses of Mexican-Americans and Indians.[55]

Thus the slave and peonage systems persisted in the region during and after the Civil War, for as late as 1866, the baptismal records show that Navahos were yet being held in a state of indentured servitude in southern Colorado and New Mexico. Below are some such entries from the records of Holy Trinity Parish which is adjacent to the present New Mexican state line near Trinidad, Colorado:

[p. 174] December 15, 1867. Rafael Navajo of five years del Senor Felipe Vaca. Godparents—Pedro Vaca and Maria (?) Vigil. Vermare. [Listed in index under Anonymous.]
[p. 186] June 11, 1868—son of Felipe Vaca [name of child not legible] and Marie Dolores Gonzales Navajo. Vermare.
[p. 188; date illegible] Maria Francesca, Daughter of Maria Antonia, Navajo, father unknown. Vermare. [Name of Vigil added later.]

[p. 191; date illegible] Felipe Neria Navajo [Cimarron] son of
Divulina Navajo, father unknown. Vermare. [Anonymous]
[p. 191] Aug. 20, 1868. Joachim Navajo born July 20, son of
Navajo parents. [Cimarron] Vermare. [Anonymous.][56]

Although peonage was largely eradicated by the decade of
the seventies, in some instances Indians continued to be held as
slaves until the early twentieth century. For example, in 1916 one
of the Indian slaves of Senator Casimiro Barela attempted to leave
his hacienda in the town of Barela (named for the owner). Outraged, Barela tried to make an example of the slave by whipping
him on the main street of the town. Things turned out quite dif-
ferently when the slave seized the whip and commenced to flog
Barela. Officials arrested the Indian, but charges were dropped
and he was freed by Barela who did not want a public record
made of the incident.[57]

By the 1880s the enslavement of the Indians was even more
subtle than in the mid-nineteenth century. The intermarriage of
Indians with Mexican-Americans and Anglos resulted in offspring
whose names did not reflect their Indian background, making it
more difficult for judicial officials to take the necessary action to
free them. The Homestead Act fostered the continuance of the
institution, as the large landowner would have some of these persons whom he held in virtual slavery file for a piece of government
land under the law.[58] As soon as the title had been perfected, the
land would be immediately transferred to the master, usually without payment, or the payment would be a credit on their "debts."
Undoubtedly, some landholdings were developed in this fashion.[59]

Because of the persistence of the peonage system and the institution of Indian slavery, socioeconomic conditions among the
masses continued to be of a degrading nature. But most ricos and
Anglos desired no changes, as this social, economic, and political
structure enabled them to maintain their positions of power.

PART III
THE COMING OF
THE ANGLOS

The Santa Fe Trail

The Hazards of the Trail

After 1821, as a result of the initiative of William Becknell who opened the Santa Fe Trail, the geographic orientation of New Mexico was towards the United States. At best theretofore the lines of communications to the south had been tenuous, for in addition to deserts, the traveler had to contend with the fierce Apaches who acted as a barrier to travel between old and New Mexico until the 1880s. Thus, New Mexicans developed a unique culture, as the Pueblos had in the past, both people being divorced from their kinsmen to the south.[1] Moreover, to the south there were no bridges, no places of refuge, and the roads were in the same sad condition as in the sixteenth century.[2] In addition, the distances were so great that under ideal circumstances it took twenty-six days for a letter mailed in Santa Fe, New Mexico, to reach Chihuahua and forty more days for the same missive to arrive at Mexico City. General George Sibley related that while in Santa Fe he did not receive a letter mailed in Mexico City on December 3, 1825, until February 26, 1826—an elapsed time of eighty-three days.[3] The people in St. Louis knew of the Mexican Revolution of 1845 much

---

*This essay first appeared in *El Palacio,* the magazine of the Museum of New Mexico, and is reprinted with the permission of the editors.

sooner than the inhabitants of Santa Fe.[4] As Lansing Bloom, renowned historian of New Mexico, has noted, the New Mexicans were truly isolated from Mexico and played little part in Mexican national affairs.[5]

The possibility of acquiring new commodities induced the people of the Spanish borderlands to welcome the opening of the Santa Fe Trail and turn their eyes from Chihuahua to the sources of such goods in Missouri. Thus the "Trail" remained the route of communications, linking together the "States" and New Mexico from 1821 until the coming of the railroad in the seventies.

Even with modern transportation facilities, the journey across Kansas is monotonous and thus a trying experience. Yet each year the wagon trains rolled across the barren plains laden with the goods which the traders hoped would result in great profits, driven by the teamsters who yearned for the romantic sounds of the strange, musical language and gay laughter to be heard in the plaza at the end of the trail.

The more famous trail ran from Independence, Missouri, across Kansas, north of the Arkansas River to Bent's Fort, constructed in 1834, thence through Raton Pass into New Mexico. It measured eight hundred miles in length. An earlier trail followed the same route to either the Cimarron or Upper Crossing on the Arkansas River and then southward to New Mexico. This road reduced the distance by fifty miles but the traveler was more vulnerable to Indian attacks.

A fact overlooked in the literature on the Southwest is that the Santa Fe Trail was, culturally speaking, a two-way street, and many Mexican-Americans were as interested in acquainting themselves with the American culture in Missouri as their Anglo counterparts were intent on realizing profits in Santa Fe. Some Mexican-Americans, in a desperate effort to insure that their children would be prepared to deal with the Anglo-American invaders on more equal terms, sent them to schools in Missouri.[6] Consequently, names like Otero, Martinez, Salazar, and others with a Spanish ring appear in newspaper columns as visitors to the city of St. Louis.[8]

Although the first caravans passed over the trail in 1822, it was not until 1825 that a bill was passed in Congress at the instigation of Thomas Hart Benton (Missouri) that authorized a

Itinerario—Santa Fe Trail[7]

En que acostumbraban acampar las caravanas que transitaban de Independencia a Santa Fe, y la distancia que de uno a otro hay, segun Mr. Gregg. [Josiah Gregg, *Commerce of the Prairies*]

Lugares	Millas	Sumas
De Independencia a Boum Grove	35	
Narrows	30	65
Creek	30	95
Bridge	8	103
Jhon Spring	40	143
Council Grove	2	145
Diamond Spring	15	160
Lost Spring	15	175
Cottonwood	12	187
Turkey	25	212
Pequeno Arkansas	17	229
Cow Creek	20	249
Rio Arkansas	16	265
Walnut	8	273
Ask Creek	19	292
Pawnee Fork	6	298
Covn Creek	33	331
Caches	36	367
Vado del Arkansas	20	387
Sand (dejando el Arkansas)	50	437

Lugares	Millas	Sumas
Rio Cimarron	8	445
Middle Arroyo	36	481
Willow Bar	26	507
Upper Spring (arroyo de arriba)	18	525
Cold Spring (arroyo frio)	5	530
M'Nee'ss	25	555
Rabbit ear (oreja de conjo)	20	575
Round Mound	8	583
Rock Creek	8	591
Point of Rocks	19	610
Rio Colorado	20	630
Ocate	6	636
Santa Clara (arroyo)	21	657
Rio de Mora	22	679
Rio Gallinas	20	699
Ojo de Bernal (arroyo)	17	716
San Miquel	6	722
Pecos (aldea)	23	745
Santa Fe	25	770
Distancia mas admitida		256

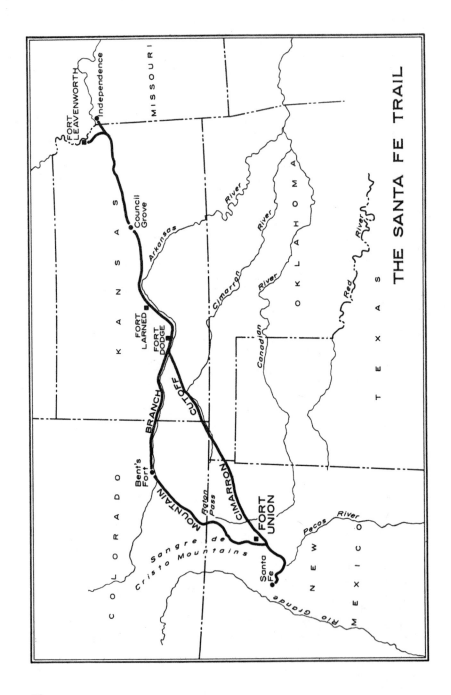

THE SANTA FE TRAIL

70

$30,000 appropriation to support the expenses of marking the trail. Subsequently, a commission that included George C. Sibley, Thomas B. Mather, and Benjamin G. Reeves was appointed to conduct the survey.[9]

The excitement generated by news of the survey was keen, and the commission was swamped with applications from adventurers desirous of participation in the project. Finally, after many delays, the party gathered at the point of departure near Independence and the great trek began on July 15, 1825. By September, the survey was completed to the line adjudged to form the boundary between New Mexico and the United States. Now, rather belatedly, the question of the Mexican government's attitude toward the conduct of the survey in their territory was raised. After some discussion it was decided that Sibley would travel to Santa Fe and consult with the governor, while Mather and Reeves would petition the Department of State to negotiate the matter with the Mexican government in an effort to arrive at an understanding.

They were disappoined in the results, for, as Sibley related, while the governor of New Mexico appeared "greatly in favor of the project," in the end the Mexican government allowed the party only to "examine the western end of the road."[10] This was frustrating, but the Mexicans remained adamant in their attitude for they were becoming increasingly aware of the threat the Anglo was beginning to pose to their position, not only in New Mexico but in Texas as well; for it was in Texas that the "aggressive gringos" were on the verge of attempting their first seizure of power that culminated in the Nagadoches incident of 1826.[11] The resultant suspicions could not help but arouse distrust of any proposal that would allow the Anglo-Americans further entry into the territory. The commissioners gave up all efforts to complete the project; instead, they retraced their steps and made some corrections in the survey that were necessitated by complaints of traders who had traveled over the trail in the past year.[12] A final review was made in 1827 before the work was declared as complete as possible under the circumstances.

The Missourians then commenced to place pressure on Benton, who was Chairman of the Senate Military Affairs Committee, to insure them army protection against the Indians. Although Congress adjourned in 1829 before action could be taken, an appeal to President Andrew Jackson resulted in Major Bennett Riley accompanying the traders the same spring. With four companies of infantry, he left Missouri on June 3, 1829, and shortly afterwards met the merchants to be escorted.[13] The troops, however, could travel only as far as the New Mexican boundary, where Riley encamped to await the return of the traders, which was expected to be on October 11. When they failed to keep the appointment, he started the return trip. A few days later, however, a messenger arrived and informed him that the merchants were on their way. He halted until they arrived before continuing the trip to Missouri.[14]

The most important result of this journey was the revelation that it was useless to send troops with the traders unless they could enter New Mexico, when the most dangerous part of the journey began. In addition, the cost of such an expedition, in contrast with the returns, was such as to make Congress reluctant to support any further enterprises of such a nature.[15]

Thus in the future, aside from a protective expedition under Captain Clifton Wharton in 1834, and one under Lieutenant James Monroe Bowman in 1839, the U.S. government refused to heed the pleas of the traders, who then turned to the state government for militia protection but this also was to no avail. Consequently, the Missouri traders were forced to prepare themselves so that not only would they be self-sufficient in food and goods but able to ward off Indian attacks. This required prodigious effort and great expense.[16]

A colorful description of the long journey was provided by a newspaper correspondent:

> I have reached Santa Fe after crossing the plains. So common that [there is] no novelty in my description for . . . there occurs the usual incidents day by day. One [is] forced to subject to the hitching up, "and unhitching," forming a "corral," and "tying up the gaps," and "untying them," "standing guard," and satisfying ourselves that the man who originated the comparison of "stubborn as a mule," must have had some experience of camp life on the plains, and having the daily knowl-

edge that a sharp appetite was easily appeased by the worst sort of cookery. Want some advice? Buy your own team and supplies rather than pay a one hundred dollar fee. Make up a party of mutual friends. The most reliable animal is the mule. It can average forty miles per day.[17]

He then suggested that Mexicans be used as teamsters for they "can catch up and roll up in half the time the average person does."

Advice to prospective travelers on the trail was offered by many persons, among them Brigham Young, who knew something about such travel:

> For the benefit of the traveling public who are intending to cross the plains the ensuing season, I have deemed that a few suggestions might be timely and profitable. . . . Men traveling . . . should consider before they start upon this journey that now . . . will be . . . brought into requisition all their forbearance, courtesy, patience, manhood, vigilance, untiring perseverance, and charitable feelings. Perhaps there is no one thing that will try a man in all these virtues equal to a trip with ox-teams across the plains. It would be well therefore not to be in a hurry, or get excited. No one should engage to make the trip in a certain number of days, for he can know but little what hindrances may interpose, what impediments he may have to overcome. Men should be careful of their supplies, part of the trip. . . . Cattle should not be hurried, nor whipped. . . . Arriving among Indians, it is sometimes the case, that emigrants shoot them without cause. They should always be treated with kindness. . . . If you trade with them do so on fair terms . . . the company should frequently look after the animals as they are like to stray from the herdsman. . . . Great care should be taken to put out your fires upon breaking up camp for it proves very injurious for such as travel the same route after you.[18]

Some of the traders were obsessed with the goal of establishing travel records across the plains. In 1846 N. Colburn, a publicity-conscious individual, reported to both the *New York Tribune* and the *Missouri Republican* that between the third and the seven-

teenth of August he made the Santa Fe–Independence run in
twenty-four and one-half days.[19] This feat, however, merely served
to whet the appetite of others for the honor of being "number
one." The most famous and undisputed champion was Francis
Xavier Aubry, merchant, trader, sheep owner, and quite possibly
the most glamorous figure of the Santa Fe Trail. In the spring of
1848 this adventurer announced that by taking short cuts at the
risk of life he would arrive at Independence in ten days. The editor
of the *Santa Fe Republican* confidently predicted that "if energy
and perseverance can accomplish a feat of that kind, Aubry is the
man."[20] Actually it took Aubry fourteen days to make the journey,
but that fact does not diminish the magnitude of his accomplishment, for in the process of the trip he wore out "six men, three
horses, and two mules," and was slowed by the fact that he had
to walk forty miles when he lost his last horse. Also, there were
times when he had to avoid the most direct route because of the
threat of Indians.[21] As amazing as was this performance, even
more astonishing was Aubry's accomplishment in September of the
same year when he made the trip in five days and sixteen hours!
This time the intrepid individual used up six horses, swam flooded
streams, and walked twenty miles.[22]

Another individual whose audacity commands respect was
a traveler identified simply as Rippetoe. In the summer of 1851
he left Mora, New Mexico, after refusing to pay what he considered
to be the exorbitant fee charged to travel with a train. Mounted on
a pony, Rippetoe made it to Ft. MacKay in Kansas on a badly worn
animal. Following a brief rest, he then took off for the Little Arkansas River only to find it in a swollen state. In his efforts to
cross the torrent, Rippetoe suffered the loss of his pony, gun, ammunition, and food. Alone, shaken by exposure, and without food,
he yet made it to Independence eighteen days after leaving Mora.[23]

Under ideal conditions it took the average person from thirty
to thirty-five days to complete the trip. In 1857 Governor Abraham Rencher made the journey from Westport, Kansas, to Ft.
Union, eighty miles northeast of Santa Fe, in twenty-eight days
and judged it to be a very fast trip.[24] There were, however, instances of frustrating delay. In a message to the legislature, Acting
Governor W. W. H. Davis urged that body to aid him in improving

movement over the trail, complaining that it took three months for a message to reach him from Washington.[25]

In addition to hostile Indians, the hazards on the trail included the fickle behavior of nature. In times of dry weather, for example, the traders constantly had to be wary of the terrifying prospects of prairie fires. In the aftermath of such a catastrophe, traders reported seeing the carcasses of horses, oxen, and buffalo along the trail, victims of the fires.[26] At times, the Indians deliberately burned the grass. In 1846 Major William Gilpin was almost forced to turn back with his entire force because of the lack of pasture resulting from fires set by the Indians. As it was, he made it to Santa Fe only after suffering numerous travails.[27]

In addition, the travelers were harassed by the threats of rain and subsequent floods. The most severe hardships were those encountered by travelers who found themselves beset by the ravage of winter. Many, indeed, were the tales of suffering and loss resulting from being trapped on the plains by snowstorms accompanied by terrific winds. The men sought shelter under the wagons, leaving the cattle in the enclosure formed by the wagons where they soon perished. As one survivor recalled of a journey in 1852:

> The snow drifted into the wagons through every crevice until they were filled nearly to the top of the bows; this fortunately sheltered the men beneath from the piercing cold without. Two of the men ventured, about daylight, to get out of their wagon for the purpose of kindling a fire, but in a few minutes became so stiffened with the intense cold, that they were unable to get into their wagon again without assistance. The others prudently kept beneath their blankets and canopy of snow during the whole day and succeeding night, not venturing to change their position, wisely determining to endure the pangs of hunger rather than run the risk of sharing the same fate of their unfortunate animals.
>
> On the second day the storm abated though the cold was still intense. They ventured from their coverts to look upon the sad wreck of life around them and to think upon the awful condition in which they were placed—a condition which none can realize but those who have experienced it. Hundreds of miles from any civilized habitation, in the midst of a desert

waste producing not a stick of timber in a range of many miles, and no animal left, they seemed to be shut up by an inexorable destiny.

One consolation was left them, the train was loaded with provisions and they could use the wagons for fuel. But for this, they must all soon have perished; they were, however, enabled to sustain themselves until succor arrived in the spring.[28]

The Company of Connelly and Glasgow suffered a like fate when, after leaving late in September 1846, they were caught by an early storm and lost two hundred mules. They escaped without the loss of human life only after the exercise of maximum will and effort.[29] The members of another train trapped by snow in early 1850 were forced to burn their wagons in order to survive. The cattle all died of exposure, and the men patiently waited until fresh oxen came along from Missouri to continue the journey to Santa Fe.[30]

The troops crossing the plains between 1846 and 1861, often for the first time, were even more vulnerable to the elements than were the seasoned travelers. In one instance a Captain Koronoy and his aide, Lieutenant Abram Allen, arrived in Ft. Mann in western Kansas with pack mules drawing wagons and the officers carrying goods on their backs because they had lost many of their animals to the wintry blasts. They then begged Major William Gilpin there, who was returning to Missouri, for the loan of some mules, but he also informed them that they could occupy the room he had provided but one night. Fortunately for the desperate officers, Gilpin's aides managed to obtain a team of mules for them in the morning. They arrived in the States after being on the road for thirty-six days with but six mules of the thirty-seven they had been provided with since leaving New Mexico.[31]

The toll of human life along the trail was quite heavy. The notices of deaths of travelers are quite frequent in the newspapers. One that is particularly poignant reads as follows: "Mr. Joseph McCana died at Cottonwood on his way to Santa Fe, and was buried at Rabbit-Ear; he was traveling for his health. Scarcely one man in the several companies escaped the chills and fever."[32]

It is impossible to determine how many died as a result of starvation on the prairie. In late 1847 a party came across two dead men at the foot of a tree, from which the bark had been eaten away. Obviously they had starved to death. After burying these two, the same party encountered another group seven days on the trail that was already on half-rations. It is uncertain if they ever made it to Independence.[33]

What made men undertake the grim journey? Some went merely for the sake of adventure. The volunteers with the Army of the West crossed the trail in quest of the military fame that would enhance their political fortunes. Following the Mexican War, the ranks of politicians in Missouri and New Mexico were filled with veterans of Kearny's expeditions. The vast majority of the travelers, however, were seeking economic profits. And well they might, for the pecuniary gains increased at a fantastic rate, from $150,000 in 1828 to $5 million in 1855. In 1860, 3,033 wagons, 9,084 men, 6,147 mules, and 27,920 oxen passed over the route.[34] Small wonder, then, that they expected the pot at the end of the rainbow to be filled with gold.

6
Anglo Reaction to the Physical Environment

Climate

Anglos arriving in New Mexico between the Mexican War and the Civil War voiced differing opinions of the area. Some protested that it was not worth what it cost the government;[1] others sneered that it was a barren wasteland; some complained of its remoteness from their homes; some deplored the backward nature of the population; and still others went further, suggesting that the Mexican-Americans were an alien and inferior people. All who traveled to the newly acquired land, however, were unanimous in their praise of the climatic conditions in New Mexico, suggesting that the weather conditions were more conducive to bodily comfort and sheer physical enjoyment than any formerly encountered. One report in 1846 noted that the trip to Santa Fe was becoming fashionable as a means of restoring the shattered health of invalids.[2] William Carr Lane, the new governor to New Mexico, stated upon his arrival in 1852, "the air is so very pure, that all this bad management cannot produce sickness."[3]

One of the foremost propagandists of the salutary effects of the weather in New Mexico was W. W. H. Davis, who, upon his return to the territory in 1883 after an absence of twenty-five years, proclaimed:

But the climate is New Mexico's greatest claim; it is simply perfect, and is not equalled in any part of the world. It is pure and dry, with little dew, and no decaying vegetable matter. Fresh meat is cured by hanging it on a line in the open air; and, if you kill your dog and lay his body on your doorstep, you will not smell him; he dries up and blows away, to join good "dorgs" [sic] in a happier land. The cholera has never been able to get nearer to Santa Fe than the Arkansas River, four hundred miles away, and when it reaches that point it always turns back in disgust. The Italians have a saying, "See Naples and die"; but the invalid can truly say "See New Mexico and live," for there shattered health is restored. That country should, and I believe in time, will become a great sanitarium, whither all the states will resort, to be cured of the ills that flesh is heir to.[4]

Indeed as early as 1860 the *Missouri Republican* observed that consumptives should take the trip across the prairie just to breathe the pure, rarefied air of Santa Fe.[5] Josiah Gregg in his classic, *Commerce of the Prairies,* testified:

Salubrity of climate is decidedly the most interesting feature of the character of New Mexico. Nowhere—not even under the much boasted Sicilian skies can a purer more wholesome atmosphere be found. Bilious diseases—the great scourge of the valley of the Mississippi—are here almost unknown. Persons withered almost to mummies, are to be encountered occasionally, whose extraordinary age is only to be inferred from their recollection of certain notable events which have taken place in times far remote. A sultry day, from Santa Fe north, is of very rare occurrence. The summer nights are usually so cool and pleasant that a pair of blankets constitutes an item seldom dispensed with. The winters are long but not so subject to sudden changes as in damper climates; the general range of the thermometer, throughout the year, being from 10° to 75° above zero, of Fahrenheit.[6]

A second health attraction in New Mexico was the presence of a number of hot springs. One observer boasted, "Besides the virtues of our Vegas, Jemez and Socorro Hot Springs are becoming ap-

parent to those afflicted with rheumatism and cutaneous diseases."[7]
One government official noted that the Kivez Hot Springs were
possessed of "powers of a highly currative [sic] character in diseases
of a cutaneous or rheumatic character."[8]

Economic Potential

But it was the economic potential that most attracted Anglos
to the territory. They were persuaded that possibilities for wealth
existed—if only the Mexican-Americans could be induced to adapt
themselves to the "Anglo-Saxon institutions and spirit, which have
given so much character to the race."[9] As one commentator observed,

> New Mexico though widely different from any portion of
> the United States in soil and climate, possesses some great ad-
> vantages from its mineral wealth, its adoption to stock and
> wool raising, and its equidistant position between the United
> States and the Californias, being a sort of connecting link.
> Its mineral wealth is but slightly developed and our attention
> will of course be directed to this important branch so little
> understood and generally so badly managed.[10]

Thus in addition to the money to be made from trading and
agricultural activities, Anglos were also attuned to the economic
opportunities present in mining and sheep raising.

The Mexican War resulted in a boom in trade, for even as
the Army of the West was en route to Santa Fe, wagons from Missouri were entering the territory laden with cotton goods that
included coarse and fine cambrics, calicos, domestic shawls, handkerchiefs, steamloom shirtings, and hose. One might also find
woolen goods consisting of super blue, stroudings, pelisse cloth
and shawls, crepes and bambazette along with silk shawls, light
cutlery items, looking glasses, and a variety of other articles included in the wares that were carried to Santa Fe.

With the outbreak of the Mexican War, the traders, unlike
their predecessors, had to make careful arrangements before leaving Missouri. Above all, they had to ensure that they were pro-

vided with quarters and store space during their stay in Santa Fe.
The man to whom many of them directed such requests was Manuel Alvarez, who in 1846 was United States consul in Santa Fe
as well as a leading businessman. Traders interested in obtaining
choice sites for use as retail outlets directed letters such as the
following to Alvarez:

> Thinking we may have some difficulty in procuring a
> good stand that is a store in a central situation, we have taken
> the liberty to ask the favour of you to try and rent us for six
> months with the privilege of continuing, one of the following
> stores if they can be had, the store occupied by the Blumners,
> if it has a back room and is for rent, next the store occupied
> by Mr. Shutz would suit us very well, next the store occupied
> by Dr. Waugh [?] or the store formerly occupied by Messervy
> would suit, the rent to commence on the arrival of our goods
> in Santa Fe. We expect to leave here in a few days and hope
> to have the pleasure of seeing you in the month of July.[11]

Oftentimes Alvarez was the landlord for the traders, occupying as he did large quarters on the plaza. On one occasion he
rented three rooms in his house for thirty-five dollars a month.[12]
Sometimes the traders might even buy property if the price was
right and then sell it after the conclusion of the seasonal business.
These holdings brought extraordinarily high sums by mid-nineteenth century standards, ranging in price from $1,200 to $4,000.[13]

Once the arrangements for business sites at Santa Fe were
completed, the wagons would make the long journey across the
trail (see Chapter 5). Before the conquest, the most formidable ob-
stacle facing the traders after this journey was the collector of customs, for the rates were so high in the eyes of the Missourians as
to constitute a gross injustice. They were even higher in 1846 on
the eve of the conflict with Mexico, as the collector, Francisco
Garcia Conde, not only charged seven dollars and fifty cents per
wagon but also one hundred and fifty dollars for "translating in-
voices." In addition, it was common for certain goods, such as
coarse cotton items, to be seized as contraband and sold at auction
by the officials. Despite these harassments, the traders predicted

in 1846 that trade would be "very prosperous" since the people in the Rio Abajo wished to make purchases.[14]

One reason for the high rates charged by the Mexicans was that the government of New Mexico was completely dependent on the fees collected from traders to support itself. One historian has observed that for ten years prior to the arrival of Kearny, the "fiscal year had been shaped by the arrival of the annual caravan across the plains," as the minutes of a session of the Departmental Assembly reveal:

> As the arrival of the United States caravan was about due—the time for payment of salaries on the list of civil officers—Donaciano Vigil moved that a committee be named to secure from the treasurer's office a statement of the advances which had been made to the Assembly for their secretary and other employees for the year past down to date, in order that an estimate might thereby be made of the credit due each one, as also the expenses of office and any other extraordinary expenses.[15]

According to one report, the duties collected in 1845 came to $105,757 on $342,530 worth of goods.[16]

After the encounter with the customs agents, the caravan drew close to Santa Fe, whereupon a state of feverish activity developed both in the city and among the traders. A typical scene was described by Josiah Gregg:

> The arrival of the caravan was productive of great excitement among the inhabitants, "Los Americanos!" "Los Carros!" "La entrada de la caravans" were to be heard in every direction. Crowds of women and boys flocked around to see the newcomers, while crowds of leperos hung about as usual to see what they could pilfer. The wagoners were by no means free from excitement on this occasion. Informed of the "ordeal" they had to pass, they had spent the previous morning in "rubbing up"; and now they were prepared, with clean faces, sleek combed hair and their choicest Sunday suit, to meet the "fair eyes" of glistening black that were sure to stare at them as they passed. There was yet another preparation to

be made in order to "show off" to advantage. Each wagoner must tie a brand new "cracker to the lash of his whip," for on driving through the streets and the *plaza publica* everyone strives to outvie his comrades in the dexterity with which he flourishes his favorite badge of authority.[17]

Once the welcome was over, the traders would unload their goods in the places of business that had been bought or rented.

The average Missourian normally invested about one thousand dollars in his goods, which usually served as collateral for the sum obtained to purchase these goods. If he was fortunate, the trader would sell his stock in Santa Fe at a sufficiently high rate of profit to enable him to pay off the mortgage and realize a sizeable return. If, however, he failed to sell his goods in·the capital city, he would continue on to Chihuahua selling goods in the Rio Abajo country along the way; or he might choose to spend the winter at Santa Fe—if his creditors were possessed of sufficient patience. A third alternative was to entrust the unsold goods to an individual such as Alvarez for later sale at higher prices.[18]

The years between 1846 and 1861 saw the trade boom. In 1846, thirty-year veteran of the trail Dr. David Waldo reported that total sales amounted to $937,000.[19] In 1855 total sales of all goods in New Mexico increased to a record high of $5 million. Among the traders who reaped substantial profits were Leitensdorfer, Hough, Glasgow, Magoffin, Branham, Connelly, Clark, Waldo, McCoy, Aubrey, Spayer, Morris, Flourney, Courtney, McKnight, Ferguson, and Colburn.

There were, however, those who failed. Some, in their economic distress, found temporary employment by utilizing a special skill—in one instance, cigar-making.[20] Others, such as H. Gosselin, turned their eyes to a second land of opportunity—California. Facing bankruptcy in 1853, after spending the winter in New Mexico, he departed and left Alvarez the following message:

> As I am about to leave for California I feel it my duty to inform you of the same. You are well aware of my present situation, necessity alone can oblige me to leave at such a critical moment. My first object is to try my luck in some other quarter as it has now become an impossibility for me

to make a decent living. . . . Should the Almighty give me a hand, I shall be most happy to return and square up with all my creditors.[21]

There were also those who concluded that the territory was an economic wasteland. Among these was the military commander in 1852, Colonel E. V. Sumner, who stated in a report to the Secretary of War:

> The truth is, the only resource of the country is the government money. All classes depend upon it, from the professional man and trader down to the beggar. Before we took the country, a considerable part of the population earned a scanty livelihood at the mines; but this work was abandoned directly when the government money was scattered broadcast among them. These mines are not productive, and never can be made so, in comparison to the inexhaustible mines of California; but a part of this people managed to earn at them a few shillings a day, and that supported them. They will be obliged to return to this work again, as it is the only means of living, while the rest must get from the soil the few articles that are necessary for their subsistence. There can never be any profitable agriculture in this country. There is but a very small part of it that is arable land; the valleys of the few streams comprise the whole of it; and much of this cannot be cultivated, owing to the efflorescence of salt; and the residue requiring such labor and kind of irrigation and cultivation that corn cannot be raised here for less than a dollar a bushel. But even if it could be raised as cheap as it is in Missouri, there would be no market for it beyond the wants of the government; and no agricultural product would ever pay transportation from this remote country.[22]

Sumner could so little hope in improved conditions that he actually suggested that all troops and civil officers be withdrawn and the Mexican-Americans left to fend for themselves as they did under the Mexican government.

Charles Conrad, secretary of war, was sufficiently impressed by Sumner's evaluation to look at the matter in a cold business fashion; he then made the following estimate of the situation:

By the last census, the total population of New Mexico
exclusive of wild Indians is (in round numbers) 61,000 souls
and its whole real estate estimated at (in round numbers)
$2,700,000. To protect this small population we are com-
pelled to maintain a large military force at an annual expense
nearly equal to half the value of the whole real estate of the
Territory. Would it not be better to induce the inhabitants to
abandon a country which seems hardly for the inhabitants of
civilized man, by remunerating them for their property, in
money or in lands situated in more favorable regions? Even if
the Government paid for the property quadruple value, it
would still, merely on the score of economy, be largely the
gainer by the transaction; and the troops now stationed in
New Mexico would be available for the protection of other
parts of our own and the Mexican Territory.[23]

Almost immediately, despite receiving some support from
Secretary of State Daniel Webster, Conrad was roundly denounced
by the Missouri traders and Mexican-Americans. The *Santa Fe
Gazette* best expressed the reaction of the people of the territory
in 1853 when it editorialized:

That such a proposition could have been conceived in
this enlightened age, will test the credulity of the historian—
that it should find favor in the estimation of any, will be a re-
proval to the intelligence of the age. Are we not standing on
American soil? Has it been purchased with the blood and
treasure of a patriot people? Are the laws of a free country
extended over us? Are we entitled to the rights of American
citizens? Can we claim the protection of freemen? No. We
are vassals of a wise and far-seeing secretary to be kept or
sold off, like the negroes on a sugar farm, in accordance with
the rise or fall in the governmental thermometer of profit and
loss. Has it come to this?—an American citizen can be protected on American soil, if it costs the government nothing to
protect him; otherwise he must quit the home of his childhood, listen no more to the song of his mountain goatherds,
and bid a last farewell to the graves of his fathers' fathers. We
are to be carried off like felonous criminals, to the lowest
bidder, or to be driven off like a herd of naked savages, to

a country "fit for the inhabitation of civilized man," because
it costs something to protect us here![24]

The editor next reminded Conrad that the Treaty of Guadalupe Hidalgo guaranteed the people that they would be permitted
to "continue where they now reside." Further, they were to be
maintained and protected in the "free enjoyment of their liberty
and property." Instead, continued the *Gazette,* the people of New
Mexico had been subjected to a military government that had failed
to live up to the guarantee of protection against the Indians, resulting in the loss of numerous lives and over two million dollars in
property. In addition, it was charged that Conrad had overlooked
the positive aspects of the territory. He ignored the flocks that
were raised and the "vines that were second to none; the blessings
of an ideal climate that was the envy of all that resided in less
healthy environment."

And yet, the editor continued, the people who had conducted
a struggle for two hundred years to remain in the territory were
being treated like "stepchildren." For example, despite the large
population of New Mexico, Minnesota with but 16,192 people
received $10,000 for geological surveys while nothing was allotted
to the government at Santa Fe. Moreover, Minnesota had been
given two townships of federal territory for support of education
while no such grant was made New Mexico; and $40,000 was allo-
cated to Minnesota for roads, twice as much for public buildings,
and three times that sum for legislative needs. As if that was not
enough, despite the pressing needs of New Mexico, Minnesota
received $60,000 for the operation of its Indian agency, while the
superintendent of Indian affairs in New Mexico was granted but
$20,000 to deal with a much more severe Indian problem.

And now the final humiliation was to be heaped on the New
Mexicans. They were to be abandoned after suffering the loss of
thirty thousand square miles of territory (to Texas). The editor
concluded that New Mexico needed a Burke or a Fox in Congress
to defend the rights of the people and to remind the nation of the
vast wealth of the territory that was yet to be exploited.[25]

There were those Anglos, however, who shared the views of
Sumner and Conrad. One recent arrival in Santa Fe declared that

the truth is that the whole country is not worth a good regiment of soldiers. It is fit for nothing but black Mexicans —white people can't live there as white people. I am told by intelligent men, who have seen the whole of New Mexico that it is the poorest country that they have ever seen.[26]

Some members of Congress echoed such sentiments, charging that the entire region was a "worthless province." Some wanted to return the area to Mexico while retaining control of California.[27] In addition, Governor Rencher did not help matters in 1859 when he wrote, "not one hundredth part of the land surveyed will be taken up or can be occupied."[28] However, the Federal government did not abandon the region. Congress, spurred on by the Missouri delegation whose constituents had such a financial stake in the territory, provided sufficient funds to support continued occupation of the territory.[29]

Army and the Economy

The army played a key role in the economy of New Mexico following the conquest. The need for goods and services was accelerated as a result of the continued presence of a great number of troops. The stimulus that was thus provided to the economic life of New Mexico helps to further explain the great power wielded by the army until after the Civil War, for from the moment Kearny entered New Mexico, merchants took advantage of the new market for their goods.

In October 1846, N. Colburn left for Santa Fe with a train of nineteen wagons laden with goods for the army at the same time that the Kean and Hall Company led a string of nine wagons filled with goods to be sold to the same troops[30]; in 1847 Alexander W. Doniphan's forces bought $4,000 worth of goods from Missouri traders in one day.[31] The payroll carried across the plains to Santa Fe on one occasion in 1847 amounted to $300,000, with most of it being spent in the territory.[32] Between government purchases and personal troop expenditures, prosperous days were experienced by the merchants. By 1852 military expenditures averaged over $3 million a year, and all classes were dependent on "government money."[33] Moreover, employment was increased with one thousand civilians being employed to construct Fort Union.[34]

Physical changes also took place in Santa Fe as a result of the coming of the army. A sawmill was built on the banks of the Santa Fe River with a grist mill being constructed soon afterwards. New buildings were erected in the town in such great number as to cause one reporter to comment:

> When General Kearny, nearly two years ago entered Santa Fe, at that time there was but one public house in the place, and it was [so] badly kept, and supplied, that but few paid a second visit.—Now we have several; the U.S. Hotel, the Santa Fe House, now kept by Americans, who have their wives and families here. Also the Missouri House and one or two private boarding houses, the tables of which, are well supplied, and one which the vegetable potatoes are only missed.
>
> The merchants have fitted up large and convenient rooms in place of small and crowded ones, and the doors, windows and other marks of improvement that strike the eye everywhere indicates a most rapid improvement.—The ruins of old houses which were scattered all over the town, have given place to new and better built ones, and as fast as workmen and materials can be procured, new buildings are going up. Not a street in the place presents the appearance it did this time two years ago, and if things continue, in one year alone the whole appearance of the city will be changed. Everything at present is quiet. . . . We often hear it remarked by young men now attached to the army, that they have a desire to settle in this country. . . . Spring has opened, business is improving, and everything denotes a lively and busy season. Citizens are sowing and planting large crops, building new and repairing up their old houses. Americans and Capitalists are purchasing building lots and garden plots. New houses are going up in every part of the city. Merchants are about arriving from the States and we believe that Santa Fe never saw the same spirit manifested, nor the same hum of every kind of business it does at present.[35]

So dependent were the merchants on the army that when Col.

Edwin V. Sumner decided in 1851 to move the troops to Fort Union in New Mexico, consternation took place among the business classes who faced financial catastrophe. "Dull, dull, dull, days of glory gone forever. Army left and things unbelievably dead," reported one trader in a letter in the fall of 1851.[36]

Their fears were in large measure unfounded as business improved when merchants bought land close to Fort Union for the purpose of supplying the troops with all of their needs from liquor to women, and the troops on leave traveled to Santa Fe where they promptly spent their pay. Also, the commissary continued to buy foodstuffs for the troops from local merchants. In 1858, for example, the army purchased two thousand head of cattle at Santa Fe.[37]

Moreover, when Albert Sidney Johnston led an American regiment against the Mormons in 1858, he found he could only obtain supplies for his men in New Mexico. In one instance, his agent purchased sixteen hundred mules and thirty wagons filled with supplies.[38] Thus, by 1861, the army was accepted as an economic force of great proportion, with the Anglos and ricos realizing almost all of the financial benefits. Except for brief employment, there was little provided the masses from the army largesse.[39]

PART IV
THE CULTURAL
CONFRONTATION

Anglo Reactions to the Mexican-Americans— The Outsiders Looking in

Anglo Reactions to Mexican-Americans

In his seminal study, *North from Mexico,* Carey McWilliams makes the observation that from the moment of first contact in Texas during the 1820s, Anglo-Americans considered Hispanos (or Mexican-Americans) to be "lazy, shiftless, jealous, cowardly, bigoted, superstitious, backward and immoral." On the other hand, to the Hispanos, Anglos were "arrogant, overbearing, aggressive, conniving, rude, unreliable, and dishonest."[1] Moreover, as both McWilliams and Leonard Pitt have shown, Anglo-Americans in California felt a "measureless contempt" for all things Mexican.[2] In all probability the Hispanos of New Mexico were equally myopic.

It should be noted, however, that the antagonisms of the Hispanos were in response to the contemptuous attitude of the conquering Anglos who felt that the confrontation between the two ethnic groups represented a contest between "barbarism and civilization." The Anglos felt that these "alien and inferior people" must conform to the Anglo concept of progressive development, if they were to be successfully incorporated into the "American system," and not remain "foreigners." The Hispanos resisted the change and failed to live up to the Anglo expectations. Thus, it is quite possible that the cultural cleavages would not have been formed had the Anglos been less disdainful in their treatment of Hispanos. Equally tragic is the fact that in the aftermath of their lands being overrun by Anglos, the desire of some Hispanos to preserve their power caused many of them to be overly cooperative with t : invaders. Consequently, the partnerships that were sometimes formed between ricos and Anglos not only occasioned a new surge of exploitation of the masses, but also further exacerbated the traditional class differences between the peons and elitists. Hence, the more privileged Hispanos and Anglo-Americans felt justified in treating the masses as second-class citizens—a condition that has persisted to the present day. The Santa Fe Ring in New Mexico, a combination of prominent Hispanos and Anglo lawyers organized to expand their landholdings at the expense of poor Mexican-Americans, was the best example of this unholy alliance between insiders and outsiders.[3]

Indeed, it was in New Mexico that Anglos most obviously displayed their contempt of Hispanos in the aftermath of the conquest of the territory in 1846. And no one more lucidly reflected this scorn than Senator Lewis Cass of Michigan, during a debate over the question of the wisdom of annexing New Mexico, when he declared:

> The senator Calhoun . . . has submitted many sound observations respecting the diversity of character, of races and of institutions, which exist between us and Mexico, and he deprecates . . . the union of the Mexican people and ours. I fully agree, sir; in all that. It would be a deplorable amalgamation. No such evil will happen to us in our day. *We do not want the people of Mexico, either as citizens or subjects.* All we want is a portion of territory . . . with a population, which would recede, or identify itself with ours. (Author's italics)[4]

Senator Cass's attitude reflected the overwhelming mass of Anglo-American public opinion regarding the Hispanos in 1846. Yet there are many scholars who still insist that the cleavages which today separate Mexican-Americans from Anglos were not present in New Mexico until the period following the invasion of the braceros in the twentieth century. Even such an acknowledged authority as Nancie Gonzalez states:

> During the early decades after the conquest there is little evidence that the Mexican population was looked down upon or discriminated against on the basis of their ethnic differences per se. Intermarriage between Anglo men and Mexican women was apparently quite common and not restricted to any particular social class. Business and commercial mergers between Anglos and Mexicans occurred frequently, and . . . Anglos and Mexicans worked together in each of the major parties. The original constitution of the state explicitly provided for the protection of the rights of the Spanish-speaking population.[5]

There is good evidence, however, to show that the contrary is true: that most Anglos from the moment of first contact were disdainful of the Hispano; that whatever intercourse occurred between the two races was usually on Anglo terms; that intermarriage was not a common phenomenon, but rather restricted to marriage between Hispano elitists and Anglos designed to serve their common economic and political interests, just as commercial or business relations between the Hispanos and Anglos served to the mutual advantage of both groups at the expense of the masses. The constitutional guarantees mentioned by Gonzalez were achieved only because the legislature was overwhelmingly Mexican-American.

Anglo-Americans frequently voiced their feelings of superiority over Hispanos; their contempt for this "inferior" culture and its institutions can be seen in the remarks of one observer who charged that there was no educational system and, "a lack of 'mechanical bonds'; rudeness of agricultural implements; wealth lost by Indian depredations; want of industry; consequent vice and immorality resulting from idleness; a wretched political system unable to afford protection and encourage capital investment and the development of even a single source of wealth."[6]

J. R. Bartlett, commissioner of the Mexican border survey,

was so repelled by the living conditions in one village that he "sent the train and party a mile beyond the village, to encamp . . . where the men would be away from the contaminations of a low Mexican population, miserable, filthy, and poor as this was."[7] Major James Carleton was even more denigratory in his description of the Mexican-American socioeconomic environment when he stated in a report:

> The dirty little villages through which we have passed, as well as those we have seen in a distance, have generally turned out their inhabitants en masse to get a sight of us. This gave us a sight of them. Had we been painters, it doubtless would have been an interesting one; for men, women, and children — mostly assemblages — exhibited themselves in groups picturesque, as well· as grotesque. . . . Indolence, squalid poverty, filth and utter ignorance of everything beyond their cornfields and acequias, seem to particularly characterize the inhabitants . . . we could but observe among them what seemed to be a universal proclivity for rags, dirt, and filthiness in all things.[8]

Because the Anglos believed that the Mexican-Americans lived in conditions of filth and squalor, they cringed at the very thought of close association with such a degraded people;[9] one Anglo suggested that Americans should "praise providence they were not born Mexicans."[10]

The Anglo-American also had low opinions of the character of the Mexican-Americans. Charles Bent, in a letter to Alvarez, charged:

> There is no stability in these people, they have no opinion of thare [sic] own, they are entirely governed by the powers that be, they are without exception the most servile people that can be imagined. They are Completely at the will of those in Power . . . let those be so Ignorant as may be they dair [sic] not express an opinion to that of thar [sic] rules, they are [not] fit to be a free people, they should be ruled by others than themselves.[11]

Josiah Gregg was equally as extreme in his evaluation of Mexican-Americans:

> The New Mexicans appear to have inherited much of the cruelty and intolerance of their ancestors, and no small portion of their bigotry and fanaticism. Being of a highly imaginative temperament and of rather accommodating moral principles—cunning, loquacious, quick of perception and sycophantic, their conversation frequently exhibits a degree of tact —a false glare of talent eminently calculated to mislead and impose. They have no stability except in artifice; no profundity except for intrigue; qualities for which they have acquired an unenviable celebrity. Systematically cringing and subservient while out of power, as soon as the august mantle of authority falls upon their shoulders, there are but little bounds to their arrogance and vindictiveness of spirit.[12]

Though attributing some good qualities to the Mexican-Americans, Gregg qualified this admission by suggesting that they were charitable, not because of sympathy for the poor, as much as from fear of the Church; possessed of some courage, inured as they were to hardship, and polite, because of the service conditions that were their lot.[13]

The Anglos were equally critical of the morals of the Mexican-Americans. Colonel E. V. Sumner, the military commander and acting governor in 1853, gave this summary:

> The New Mexicans were thoroughly debased and totally incapable of self-government, and there is no latent quality about them that can *ever* make them respectable. They have more Indian blood than Spanish, and in some respects are below the Pueblo Indians; for they are not as honest or as industrious.[14]

The Anglos became even more critical following the Taos Rebellion of 1847. The reporter for the *Missouri Republican* was quite bitter in his estimate:

A country with but few exceptions is inhabited by ignorant, dishonest, treacherous men; and women who are believed scarcely what virtue is beyond the name, is now part
of the American Union! Are they worthy of a protection
against the Indians?[15]

A month later this correspondent was still writing in the
same vein:

Here is naturalization on a grand scale. But what a
blessed collection of voters. Not one in five hundred will
know anything of the size, form, locality, arts, commerce or
interests generally of the United States. Such are our new
fellow citizens. Very few, indeed, can read or write and the
most intelligent have no clear or accurate ideas of our
country.

Verily, "annexation" of such a horde of barbarians and
slaves, is a novelty in our history. I say slaves for a large proportion of the Mexican population are actually slaves, though
not in the same sense in which we use the term in the United
States.[16]

Bartlett thought the Hispano was also a corrupting influence
on the "wild Indian":

Near by [in southern New Mexico] is a fertile valley, a
very small portion which is now tilled: although from appear-
ances, it was all formerly irrigated and under cultivation ... A
more thoroughly lazy set of people I never saw. The Pimo
and Coco-Maricopa Indians of the Gila, are infinitely superior
to them. Whether a proximity to the church and the worthless
half-civilized Mexicans had reduced them to this state of
indolence and poverty, I know not; but if so, they would better
have remained in their native valleys.[17]

Other voices flung other charges. The average Mexican-
American was viewed as backward and possessed of "low morals."[18]
He was nothing more than a low "greaser"[19] and so "mongrel and
motley as to be impossible of salvation."[20] He was incapable of
appreciating "human liberty and progress,"[21] and was a product

of the promiscuous intercourse between Spaniard and Indian that made him an "offspring of sin."[22] In fact, the "female peon gladly exchanged her effete and sensual paramour for the brutal Indian master."[23]

Manuel Alvarez, of pure Spanish extraction, joined the chorus of denunciation. Like others of his kind, he was careful to differentiate between the "mixed and unmixed" elements in the population:

> The conquistadores were a race of men as patient of toil and indifferent to danger—as full of energy and enterprise as the boldest and busiest Anglo-American as ever lived. Yet even not a trace of these characteristics is to be found in the Mexican descendants of the pure blood of Spain. There are to be sure, we suppose very few Spaniards who go to make up the population of the Mexican Empire. The race being more mingled with the native Indians.[24]

The same contemptuous attitude was present in Congress, as reflected in a speech by John C. Calhoun in 1848:

> We have conquered many of the neighboring tribes of Indians, but we have never thought of holding them in subjection or of incorporating them into our Union. . . . To incorporate Mexico would be the first departure of the kind; for more than half of its population are pure Indians, and by far the larger portion of the residue mixed blood. . . . Ours is the government of the white man. The great misfortune of what was formerly Spanish America, is to be traced to the fatal error of placing the colored race on an equality with the white. That error destroyed the social arrangement which formed the basis of their society. This error we have wholly escaped. . . .
>
> Are we to associate with ourselves as equals, companions, and fellow citizens, the Indians and mixed races of Mexico? I would consider such association as degrading to ourselves and fatal to our institutions.[25]

Edward A. Hannegan of Indiana manifested a similar disposition in his reply to those who referred to the Mexicans as descendants of the Spanish:

This argument, if it agreed with the case, would be very good; but under existing circumstances it is worth nothing. In the first place, all the information I possess teaches me that a vast majority of the Mexican people have scarcely a drop of Spanish blood in their veins. They are principally Indians and a mongrel race, with the negro stock ingrafted upon the Indian, and occasionally a mixture of Spanish. But Spaniards and their descendants do not constitute one-fifth of the entire population. So that the great proportion do not have this inherent obstinacy in conflict.[26]

Thus, Hannegan concluded, it was impossible for any amalgamation to take place:

Mexico and the United States are peopled by two distinct and utterly unhomogeneous races. In no reasonable period could we amalgamate. Nomadic in their habits, and grossly ignorant, as a vast proportion of them are, they are utterly unfit for the blessings and restraints of rational liberty, because they cannot comprehend the distinction between regulated freedom, and that unbridled licentiousness which consults only the evil passions of the human heart, making each man the avenger of his own wrongs, and government itself a mere plaything, at the capricious pleasure of the infuriated mass. With them as with our own savage tribes, is the utter absence of civil restraint of laws.[27]

After serving as acting governor of New Mexico in 1856/1857, W. W. H. Davis felt that the Hispanos had benefited from the laws of the United States, were improving in dress and manner, and were learning from the example set by the Anglo.[28] But the vast majority of the Anglo observers had little hope that the "greasers and loafers" could ever fit into the American future.[29] Such negative reactions on the part of the Anglos help to explain why New Mexico was treated like a stepchild by Congress during the territorial period. The Anglo attitude is summarized well in Bartlett's paean of self-praise:

How can any American help but feel proud of his country? How much better does he love it after witnessing the poverty, ignorance, and imbecility of another nation Mexico, and how much better satisfied is he with his own laws and institutions after an opportunity to compare them with others? No wonder that Americans who breathe such a free atmosphere should always look to their country as the best, the freest, and most happy on the face of the earth.[30]

Behavior of the Anglos

One of the immediate consequences of the Anglo feelings of smugness and superiority was a pattern of behavior in their relations with Mexican-Americans that was not only brutal and insensitive, but served to further exacerbate the ill feelings between the two ethnic groupings. Although there were rare instances of understanding of the needs and desires of the Hispanos on the part of the Anglos, the vast majority of the newcomers from the states were inclined to be haughty, quick to take offense, and contemptuous of Mexican-American custom and law. It was an attitude that would long persist.

On more than one occasion the people of southern New Mexico witnessed the Anglos taking the law into their own hands. In 1853, for example, an Anglo en route to California known only as Nager claimed to have lost forty head of cattle on the east bank (American side) of the Rio Grande near El Paso. Without consulting authorities, he crossed into Mexico and drove back to the American side not only ten head of the ones he claimed to be his, but some Mexican cattle as well. When he was arrested and jailed by the Mexican police, an Anglo mob stormed the jail, and in the melee, one person was killed and many more were injured.[31]

Santa Fe experienced several incidents of Anglo violence. In 1851 a recent arrival, W. C. Anderson, fell on an unoffending Hispano boy and mauled him to the point where the boy was senseless. As if that were not enough, Anderson pulled out a pistol, put it to the head of the youth and shot him dead. The Mexican-American population was furious but the authorities did nothing.[32]

The inhabitants of the capital city were even more incensed at the behavior of the soldiers, both volunteers and regulars, who left much to be desired in their treatment of Hispanos. Indeed, after the volunteers occupied Santa Fe, they behaved as though the Mexican-Americans were to be preyed upon rather than protected, as promised by Kearny. One reporter noted in 1846:

> Men forget the object for which they are here, and forget the position which they occupy. We have seen some of the consequences fairly before us now at Santa Fe—for I do not exaggerate at all, when I say, that not a day passes, but what some outrage, some crime is committed . . . whose victims usually are Mexicans.[33]

Charles Bent, the governor appointed by Kearny, recognized the gravity of the situation and to his credit, appealed to Colonel A. W. Doniphan, Kearny's successor, to take corrective action:

> In consequence of the numerous complaints of the insubordination and after offensive and abusive conduct of the interpose your authority and compel the soldiers to respect the troops of our command, my duty compels me to call on you to rights of the inhabitants. These outrages are becoming so frequent that I apprehend consequences may result sooner or later if measures are not taken to prevent them.[34]

Whatever the intentions of Doniphan and his successor, Sterling Price, the situation did not improve as Hispanos continued to be subjected to more abuses and were the ones "to suffer most" from the outrages committed by the troops.[35] It was useless for a Hispano to seek redress since he was considered "as occupying a station far beneath that of a negro slave."[36] The reporter for the *Missouri Republican* noted that officers were reluctant to take action against army volunteers guilty of misconduct:

> If a commander here, therefore, undertakes to but listen to any of the numerous complaints which Mexicans daily make against some of the troops, he infringes on the inviolable rights of some of those poltroons or demagogues, who have smuggled themselves into the army.[37]

By the summer of 1847 the territory was rent by violence, with the volunteers committing acts of "outrage and oppression" against all alike—"the unoffending as well as the offending." They acted in the most "insubordinate and oppressive manner, neither respecting the rights of property or persons."[38]

Some Anglos were appalled. Calling the army a "military mob," one group in 1847 voiced this complaint:

> The want of restraint has produced a degree of dissipation, and of indulgence of depraved and vicious passions, on the part of officers as well as soldiers, for which we were unprepared. Gambling and drunkedness [sic], without any attention to the discipline or the tactics of a camp, prevail all over Santa Fe.[39]

In the fall of 1847 Sterling Price temporarily returned to Missouri, leaving Colonel Edward Newby in charge of the army at Santa Fe. This officer, probably the most sensitive of the Anglo commanders, attempted to correct the abuses. He prohibited gambling, forbade the holding of fandangos, and prohibited shopkeepers from selling liquor to the troops. Moreover, assisted by Colonel Alton B. Easton, Newby tried to exercise stricter discipline in the relations between the soldiers and the civilian populace.[40] He received little cooperation from the majority of the officers, however, for they resented Newby's interference with their pleasures. The Anglo traders who were now suffering the loss of profits also attempted to frustrate the commander's attempts to correct the abuses.[41] After Price returned, troop disturbances, while not quite as violent as before, continued until the army departed for Chihuahua at the end of the year.[42]

The situation was little improved when regular troops replaced the volunteers. They displayed the same contempt towards the Hispanos as the Anglo civilians and the volunteers before them. Although the victim of the following incident was not a Mexican-American but an Indian, the episode was representative of the attitude of most Americans to the "inferior" breeds. The writer was a soldier who described the actions of a comrade following the erection of a bivouac in Indian country:

After dark a noise was heard near our camp. At first we supposed it to be an animal of some kind. Three or four of us made an examination through the willow bushes and found an Indian child which I suppose was about eight months old. It was strapped to a board as all Indian babies are. I found it. An old gruff soldier stepped up and said, "Let me see that brat." I handed it to him. He picked up a heavy stone, tied it to the board, dashed baby and all into the water, and in a moment no trace of it was left. The soldier's only comment was, "You're a little feller now but will make a big Injun bye and bye. I only wish I had more to treat the same way."[43]

Similar scenes of savagery occurred in Santa Fe. In 1850, for example, in response to a real or imaginary misdeed inflicted on one of them, a mob of soldiers commenced beating Mexican-Americans and converged on the Exchange Hotel (located on the plaza), intent on destroying that favorite meeting place. In the mad scene that followed one person was killed and many more severely injured. For days afterward tensions ran high and the fear of a mass slaughter of Mexican-Americans by the troops ended only with extraordinary measures taken by the officers.[44]

Even after many soldiers were removed from the city to Fort Union, the troops continued to act in a disorderly fashion when they visited Santa Fe. Governor Rencher in 1857 described the troops as "recruits and a very bad lot."[45] And in the same year, the Mexican-Americans were subjected to further outrage when a group of soldiers attacked a popular apothecary by the name of Gruber as he attempted to serve them. In self-defense he shot one of the soldiers and gave himself up to authorities who placed him in jail. The soldiers, bent on revenge, then stormed the jail, killed Gruber and wounded two other Mexican-Americans. No punishment was meted out to those responsible and once again the Mexican-Americans experienced the fury of frustration.[46] These humiliations and instances of mistreatment are not forgotten by Hispanos; they are included in the stories that have been passed down from one generation to the next.[47]

8

Culture and Economic Problems Following the Anglo Occupation

Introduction

Governors of the Territory of New Mexico, 1846-1861:
Charles Bent, 1846-1847, Civil Governor
Donaciano Vigil, 1847-1848, Civil Governor
Sterling Price, 1846-1848, Military Governor
John M. Washington, 1848-1849, Military Governor
John Munroe, 1849-1851, Military Governor
James S. Calhoun, 1851-1852, Civil Governor
E. V. Sumner, 1852, Military Commander acting as Civil Governor
John Greiner, Secretary, Acting Governor
William Carr Lane, 1852-1853, Civil Governor
William S. Messervy, 1853, Acting Governor
David Meriwether, 1854-1857, Civil Governor
W. W. H. Davis, 1856-1857, Acting Governor
Abraham Rencher, 1857-1861, Civil Governor

To recount the full story of the Territory of New Mexico before the Civil War one has to describe the cultural and economic problems as well as the political developments. In this chapter, however, the political history will be referred to only when necessary for clarification as it has been more than adequately treated in other works.[1]

The Problem of Illiteracy

The first governor, Charles Bent, expressed a concern with the high rate of illiteracy that existed in New Mexico. In fact, Bent's first recommendation was for the passage of a bill to sponsor the construction of schools "for a well and uneducated people about to become citizens of the United States."[2]

The Anglos were not the first to take note of the lack of educational facilities. As early as 1825, a commission appointed by the ayuntamiento that included Antonio Sena, Juan Diego Sena, and Francisco Baca y Ortiz reported that "Ignorance was rampant [in New Mexico] because there were no schools worthy of the name. The parents of children preferring to employ their boys in herding goats."[3] The report concluded that "it was to be seen that progress and the furthering of education and learning are things beyond remedy at the present time."[4] Conditions were little changed by 1846 as the only school in the territory was the one at Taos, presided over by Father Antonio Jose Martinez, which numbered from thirty-five to forty pupils drawn from the ranks of ricos.[5]

Following the successful revolt against Spain, the Mexican government in 1829 passed an act that excluded all Spanish citizens, including teachers, from the territory. This law was the major reason for the shortage of schools. Moreover, these teachers had been quite progressive and utilized the Lancastrian system of education in which monitors worked with small groups of students.[6] In addition, the many attempts at public education during the Mexican period were doomed from the start because of lack of funds.

Following Governor Bent's assassination by Mexicans and Indians during the Taos uprising in 1847, his successor Donaciano Vigil received sufficient support from various ricos to found a school. They were impressed with his warning that Mexican-Americans must be educated to prevent the Anglos from assuming all power. The school employed but one teacher, however, and was generally inadequate. Further appeals for funds fell on deaf ears because of the heavy opposition to property taxes and the opposition of the Catholic Church to public education.[7]

New Mexico would not have been averse to accepting federal aid for education, and the possibility of providing such aid was discussed in Washington. In 1847 Congressman Charles Ingersoll suggested that it was essential that "our institutions" be introduced among the "civilized half-breeds"; the "slothful superstitions, brutish people, sprinkled over great spaces must be Americanized."[8]

Despite such statements, based on an attitude of ethnic superiority, no funds for education were appropriated on either a territorial or national level between 1846 and 1851. A few sporadic efforts were undertaken, however, to operate private schools. In 1848 Don Francisco Ortiz, long a supporter of educational programs, announced the availability of "Schoolbooks," and offered his Santa Fe schoolroom to any person wishing to use it for educational purposes.[9]

After the territory was organized, Governor James S. Calhoun informed the members of the legislature that Congress had granted New Mexico the sixteenth and thirty-sixth sections of each township for educational purposes—land that included arid plains and rugged mountains and was valueless. Calhoun, however, hoped other types of financial assistance would be added to the land grants.[10]

The governor also suggested, to the amazement of the male Mexican-American representatives, that women be educated:

> I regard it as important to establish female seminaries, as to educate the women of New Mexico. Unless our females are wise and virtuous there can be no refinement in society, and men will imbrute themselves. Every interest of society demands that a proper system of education shall be established without delay.[11]

Calhoun reflected in this message not only the liberal emphasis on educational values, but the moral guardian theme, so popularized by Sarah Hale in her novels, wherein woman had to be adequately educated to perform the precious task of controlling the passions and subsequent irrational actions of the male.[12] W. W. H. Davis agreed with the need for female education, suggesting that a woman in New Mexico who could write was a rarity indeed.[13]

Calhoun's hopes were short-lived. Once again, Congress refused to appropriate any educational funds, and the rico legislature would not give financial support to public schools despite the fact that the census of 1850 showed a population of 61,547 inhabitants of whom 25,089 were illiterate. Davis felt that the illiteracy figure was too low as only 460 were enrolled in private schools in 1850.[14]

Attempts were made by religious groups and private individuals to open private schools. One of the first of these, the Santa Fe Academy, was founded by the Reverend M. Reid, a Baptist minister. Subjects taught included "ABCology, Farley's Geography, with the sublime mysteries of simple subtraction."[15] Reid made a trip to St. Louis in late 1851 to solicit funds, claiming that he had established a good school.[16]

The *Santa Fe Weekly Gazette* ridiculed Reid's claim of success. Actually, the paper declared, the Mexican-Americans did not accept Reid's school and only ten pupils were enrolled. The Spanish-speaking people wanted Mexican-American teachers instructing in the Spanish tradition. They wanted to learn to read their own language before studying the English language. Hence the editor suggested the Anglos should pay for the schools that taught English.[17]

The *Missouri Republican* supported Reid, declaring that the people had to "become true Americans" and develop a common culture even if this meant abandoning their own cultural identity. They must be able to understand "our" laws, constitution and judicial system, the editor continued. The opposition to Reid's school, the editor charged, was incited by priests who resented Reid's proselytizing Catholics into the Baptist faith.[18] In the end, his school was closed because of lack of support and a shortage of funds.

Other Protestant schools were founded in the pueblos of Taos and Laguna. Twenty-five children were enrolled at Taos,[19] but the school at Laguna, established by Samuel Gorman in 1852, was more successful despite a lack of funds, little cooperation from the Indians, and the opposition of the priests. Gorman directed this school until 1861,[20] when he departed for the States and was replaced by his able assistant, Jesus Sena, who administered the school until it was closed in 1876.

Far more successful were the efforts made by Catholics to

start schools in the territory. The fact that the population was over-whelmingly Catholic partially explains this success, but the driving force of Bishop Lamy was also an important reason. As early as 1852, he enlisted the aid of six Sisters of Loretto who founded an academy for girls which served the people until 1969.[21] In 1859 the Christian Brothers of St. John the Baptist de La Salle founded St. Michael's College (a secondary school) which remains the oldest chartered school in New Mexico. In 1947 the Brothers, who had restricted their teaching to the elementary and secondary school levels in the New Orleans–Santa Fe Province, opened a four-year college in Santa Fe.[22]

W. W. H. Davis attested to the contribution made by the re-ligious orders:

> A slight change for the better has taken place, in an edu-cational point of view, since the country fell into the hands of the United States. The boarding and day schools at Santa Fe, under the care of Bishop Lamy, will, in time, produce a good effect in the Territory. The public come from various sections of the country, who, carry with them enlarged ideas, and be the means of disseminating, to some extent, a knowl-edge of our country and institutions. They will make a new generation of youth of both sexes, and, if so disposed, can do much toward the generation of New Mexico.[23]

In addition to the efforts made by private groups, the gov-ernors continued to urge the construction of public schools. In 1853 David Meriwether pointed out that experiments conducted in the states "proved" that the high crime rate in New Mexico resulted in large measure from a lack of educational facilities. It was reasoned that if the legislature passed a bill establishing a school system, crime would be reduced in New Mexico.[24]

Once again the legislature refused to vote a property tax, but agreed to appeal to Congress for one-eighteenth of the funds re-ceived from the sale of public lands for educational purposes. But Congress would not support the proposal and no public schools were constructed. In 1856 Davis proposed that the lawmakers in Washington appropriate a set sum with the principal being invested so that territorial schools could be constructed and operated on the interest. Once again Congress refused to appropriate federal funds for the educational needs of New Mexico.[25]

Meriwether and Davis continued to apply pressure until the New Mexican Legislature agreed to a compromise bill that established a system of "common schools" to be supported by a property tax. Four counties, however, all controlled by ricos, were given the option to either accept or reject the legislation with the following results:

Counties	For the law	Against the law
Taos	8	2,150
Rio Arriba	19	1,928
Santa Ana	8	456
Socorro	2	482
	37	5,016[26]

An indignant Davis penned a protest:

> The returns show that, in a popular vote of 5,053, there were only 37 men to be found in favor of public schools, a fact which exhibits an opposition to the cause of education truly wonderful. This great enmity to schools and intelligence can only be accounted for as follows: that the people are so far sunk in ignorance that they are not really capable of judging of the advantages of education. For this result, the cause of education has but little to hope for from the popular will, and the verdict shows that the people love darkness rather than light.[27]

The entire plan collapsed and Meriwether suggested either a modification or repeal of the law. The legislature enthusiastically followed the latter course,[28] and at the same time passed an act incorporating a private academy in Albuquerque that closed within a year.[29]

Governor Rencher had the same concern for education that Meriwether had. He stated in a message to the legislature in 1857:

> I should do great injustice to this interesting occasion if I

failed to bring to your favorable notice the great cause of education. Not simply the education of the rich, by the endowment of colleges; but the education of the masses by the common schools. In a government like ours depending essentially, as it does upon public opinion, it is all important that public opinion be enlightened. Public schools . . . ought to be the first duty of every statesman and patriot, . . . it is the only means of preserving our free institutions. The donation of public land, made by Congress for the support of common schools in this territory, is not yet available, and until it can be made so, it is not expected you can do much upon this important subject. But if you can do but little it will at least be the commencement of this noble work the education of the poor.[30]

As in the past, his appeal was ignored by the legislature and once again those interested in education turned to private sources of help.

In 1858 the Joseph Institute was opened at Taos by J. H. Holmes and his wife, both formerly of New York City. Instruction for girls, conducted by Mrs. Holmes, included classes in guitar, needlework, and embroidery. Boys were taught reading, geography, arithmetic, and etiquette. Tuition, room, and board varied from $50 to $72 per term depending on age; girls paid $72 if their instruction included guitar, but were only charged $68 without the instrument.[31] The school remained open until the outbreak of the Civil War.

It was not until 1860 that a bill was finally passed that provided for compulsory public education. Under this act, teachers received fifty cents per month for each child taught. The local justices of the peace were responsible for the operation of the schools, since they appointed the teachers, inspected the classes, and removed instructors found to be incompetent.[32] Rencher optimistically observed that, "though small, it is the commencement of a good work, and enterprises of the greatest value and magnitude often [have] small beginnings."[33] The Census of 1860 indicates that the act was at least partially effective, for, although adult illiteracy increased from 25,085 to 32,785 in that year, there were six hundred pupils enrolled in four private schools, and seventeen public schools which employed thirty-three teachers. Most of the students, however, were attending the Catholic private schools.[34] Unfortunately, the Civil War brought to an end further advances, and it was not until 1891 that a system of compulsory education was permanently established in New Mexico.

The Problem of Land Titles

Surveyor Generals:
William Pelham, 1854-60
Alexander P. Wilbar, 1860
John A. Clark, 1861

The surveyor generals, who were responsible for verifying land claims, should have had a great influence on the lives of the people but actually exercised little. They supervised the validation of land titles, but because they lacked sufficient authority were unable to enforce a program that prevented illegal seizures of land by the Anglo-Americans.

The origins of the land problem in New Mexico lay in the fact that there were no vast, arable government landholdings which might be allotted to settlers. All the land of value had long been settled and parceled out to Mexican-Americans and a few Anglos as grants. The public land was either too arid or vulnerable to Indian attacks; consequently there were no sales of public land before the Civil War.

The major task of the surveyor general in the fifties was to confirm land titles and to seek congressional approval of Mexican-American and Pueblo grants. There were both town grants and individual grants; some large, others small, and all vague and indefinite. The situation was made more complex by the new American common law system which so few Mexican-Americans understood. As a consequence, prompt judicious policies were necessary to insure justice to Mexican-Americans.[35] Unfortunately, the surveyor generals lacked the legal powers which would have enabled them to enforce such policies. Hence the Anglos were later free to employ legal action to obtain vast acreage at the expense of Mexican-Americans.

In Congress some men foresaw the problem. In 1849 Representative Sidney Breese introduced a bill creating the offices of Surveyor General, Register of Lands, and Receiver of Public Money. In addition to their individual duties, these officials would sit as a board of adjucation of land claims in both California and New Mexico.[36] This vast area was considered to be too large for a single board to administer, and the bill died on the floor. An additional objection to the bill came from Senator Thomas Hart Benton who opposed a board of Anglos:

> Each claimant throughout the entire country is to come in with his title and make it good before a board to be composed of foreigners, whose language they cannot speak. Terror and Consternation will pervade the land when the Mexicans and Californios, a conquered people, a helpless people, ignorant in our language, find the very titles to their property subjected, not even to the law under which they have lived, but to the pleasure of the agent of their conquerors. How is this to act; Sir? At the first summons to appear before such a board, I say—and I say it with a knowledge of what took place under similar boards in Louisiana—terror and consternation will pervade the land.[37]

Benton predicted that the board would take the land from the Mexican-Americans. Their only appeal would be to petition Congress for redress, and this process could consume years. Benton was not entirely opposed to a board of land commissioners after the boundaries had been defined, if it included Mexican-Americans.[38]

Governor Calhoun also recognized the need for a survey and settlement of land titles. In his first message, he said that the "questionable tenure" by which property was held was a "great source of irritation in this Territory." Uncertain titles clouded the status of landed property, public buildings and property, and church property; indeed, because of the absence of fences, it was difficult to distinguish between public and private property.[39]

Not until 1854 was the office of Surveyor General established. The holder was made responsible for land surveys and sales of public land, of which each settler could claim one hundred sixty acres. None of the land claims of new settlers were recognized if they conflicted with claims approved by Congress under the Treaty of Guadalupe Hidalgo. In a sense, therefore, Congress questioned Mexican-American land claims by insisting that they be validated by Congress. Moreover, very few claims were made on the arid and apparently valueless public lands by Anglo settlers.

A fault of the bill that created the office was that it did not require its holder to be a lawyer or grant him the power to validate legal claims by Mexican-Americans. He needed legal knowledge and legal authority to deal with those Anglos who were intent on grabbing land. As an example of their activities, one C. P. Clever wrote John V. Watts, who was in Washington, and requested information on any land bills being considered, particularly those dealing with the granting of county land to volunteers who had fought the Indians in 1855/1856. He promised that Watts would be well compensated for this information. Congress, however, passed no bill dealing with New Mexican land and neither of them realized a profit.[40] This correspondence suggests that there were men in the territory who were aware of the potential profit in land speculation. Again in 1857 Watts attempted to make a profit when he wrote the Surveyor General William Pelham a confidential letter asking that some land warrants be held for him and transferred at a latter date. He also requested Pelham to purchase any available land claims for later speculation.[41] By the end of 1857 Watts was up to his neck in land dealings.[42]

Although he failed to validate Mexican-American land claims, Pelham conducted surveys of unsettled areas which might attract settlers. Included among the regions surveyed were the Rio Grande Valley, which he determined averaged thirty-five miles in width; the Jornada del Muerto, which he thought might possibly have artesian wells; La Valle Grande, forty miles northwest of Santa Fe; the Pecos and Galisteo River areas; and later with his aide, Alexander Wilbar, sections of the San Luis Valley.[43] The *New York Herald* praised Pelham as follows:

> It is also gratifying to us to find that the Surveyor-General, Wm. Pelham, Esq., is conducting the public surveys with

great energy, and that the people are locating some rich valleys in our mountain country. These lands will be located mostly under the Donation Act of 1854. This law will expire in January next; but it is certain that Congress will re-enact it during the next session.[44]

In 1860 Pelham was succeeded by Alexander Wilbar, who was immediately involved in a dispute over land titles. A Mexican-American, Juan Batista Vigil, insisted that the surveyor general was guilty of dereliction of duty under the Treaty of Guadalupe Hidalgo. He referred specifically to that article of the treaty relating to property rights which stipulated that a list of all *bona fide* land titles be drawn up. No surveyor general had complied with this requirement, Vigil charged. Vigil urged that this violation be remedied and that the United States must protect Mexican-American property in conformity with Emerich Vattel's law of nations concept. He closed his denunciation by quoting from a decision handed down in *U. S.* vs. *Rencheman* involving land titles in conquered areas: "The people change their loyalties; their relations to their old sovereigns are broken; but their relations among themselves and their property rights remain permanent."[45] Vigil anticipated and sought to ward off the threat to Mexican-American land titles.

No action, however, was taken in response to Vigil's plea. By 1861 only seventeen Pueblo land claims and nineteen private and town land claims were approved. Thus, an air of uncertainty as to the validity of land titles bred further suspicions in the minds of Mexican-Americans as to the intentions of the Anglo-Americans.

Slavery and the Black Man in New Mexico

The question of the place of the black man in New Mexico was considered as early as 1850 when an abortive constitutional convention called in the first attempt to gain statehood for New Mexico conferred citizenship only on white men. Most of the members believed that the place of black men should be a low one. Hugh Smith, the elected delegate from New Mexico who was never seated in Congress, denounced the blacks as responsible for the decay of the South.[46] Governor Calhoun in 1851 asked the legislature to bar free blacks from the Territory:

> Free negroes are regarded as nuisances in every State and Territory in the Union, and where they are tolerated, society is most degraded. I trust the legislature will pass a law that will prevent their entry into this territory. The disgusting degradation to which society is subjected by their presence, is obvious to all, and demands a prohibitory act of the severest character.[47]

The intensity of the opposition to admission of free blacks to New Mexico was nearly equaled by the desire not to allow the institution of slavery to be legally recognized. At the 1850 convention it was stipulated that:

> Slavery in New Mexico is naturally impracticable, and can never, in reality, exist here; wherever it has existed it has proved a curse and a blight to the State upon which it has been inflicted,—a moral, social and practical evil. The only manner in which this question now affects us is politically; and on grounds of this character, with its general evil tendencies, we have unanimously agreed to reject it—if forever.[48]

All of the delegates signed this statement. But as Calhoun's message indicated, the Anglos and Hispanos were not so much antislavery as they were antiblack. In fact, by 1856 the New Mexican political leaders were so opposed to blacks that the legislature passed a bill restricting the movement of free blacks into the territory, and forced those living in New Mexico to post the sum of $200 to ensure good behavior and their ability to support themselves. Moreover, a free black could not remain in New Mexico longer than thirty days and intermarriage was prohibited. Finally, newly freed blacks were ordered to leave the territory within one month of manumission.[49]

One observer complained that the law remained a dead letter in New Mexico since the masses had no prejudices against the black man. This paradox led him to express a fear of racial mixture:

The introduction of negro slavery into New Mexico, may in time seriously affect the social and domestic relations of the Territory. Among the lower classes the Mexicans know no distinction of color, and the women as soon intermarry and cohabit, with a negro as one of their own race. This evil has become so apparent, and seemed to be so much on the increase, that the legislature some time ago passed a severe law against the intermarriage of Mexicans and negroes, but the statute had little if any influence against the inclinations of the inhabitants, and the penalty was never enforced. Now if Negro slaves should be introduced into the Territory to any number, there will be an extensive intermarriage and cohabitation between them and the lower classes, and in time the negro blood will be generally diffused through the population.[50]

In another statement this man predicted, "in all that . . . region [New Mexico] now inhabited by the Mongrel Spanish race, there may be reared up a mulatto nation, which John Quincy Adams always believed would be the case some day."[51]

The introduction of negro slavery into New Mexico, may
This and other evidence indicates that the masses of Mexican-Americans had no prejudice against blacks and agreed with the Indians who were inclined to accept the negro as "a black man with the hair of the white man on his face."[52]

The Anglo-dominated government ignored the issue of slavery expansion until 1859 when Miguel Otero, New Mexican delegate to Congress, who was courting Southern support for a railroad through New Mexico, arranged for passage of a Slave Code. W. W. H. Davis related that the majority of officials were opposed to the measure:

The power of the administration was exerted against raising any question upon the subject of slavery. There was a general acquiesance on the right of the master to bring his slaves into the territory, and no legislation was deemed necessary, as a [Federal] fugitive slave law has provided for the reclamation in case of escape.[53]

Davis was consequently perturbed when the New Mexican

legislature passed the Slave Code Act of 1859, and made the following comment on the meaning of the legislation:

> We see in our exchanges, that the House of Representa-
> tives of New Mexico has passed a very stringent act upon the
> subject of negro slavery, which not only legalized it, but pro-
> vided that emancipation shall never take place. This will sur-
> prise those who honor the sentiment of the people of New
> Mexico upon this subject, and especially how illegally adopted
> by nature is the Country to Slave labor. We do not believe
> there are five hundred Mexicans in the Territory really in
> favor of the introduction of negro slavery, for the simple
> reason, if there were no others, that [they] now have a cheaper
> system of Labor in peonage than that of slavery.[54]

Davis then suggested that "present movement was a political
trick," pressured through the legislature by those in authority who
were determined to unsettle the "beautiful relations" that had
existed in New Mexico. In fact, Davis thought the Slave Code so
contrary to New Mexican interests that he predicted the next legislature might be so irrational as to pass an act "to hang the Governor of the Territory and all other federal officers."[55]

Davis was correct in his estimate of the situation for the opposition to the act was so great that a demand was made in the next
legislature for a repeal of the Slave Code. Consequently, a group
was appointed to examine and report on the matter. However, the
five prominent Mexican-Americans appointed to the committee—
Miguel A. Lobato, Manuel S. Salazar y Vigil, Candlelario Garcia,
Antonio Tafoya, and Matias Medina—all were in the Otero camp.
As a result, they presented a report that might have been written
by John C. Calhoun, which stressed the responsibility of the government to protect slaves as property in the territory and declared
New Mexico would be guilty of bad faith if she did not live up to
that responsibility. Moreover, they stated, New Mexico had been
purchased from Mexico by all of the states, including those in the
South. Thus citizens from those states were entitled to the same
treatment and privileges as citizens from other sections. Finally, on
a political note, it was pointed out that Southerners had led the

way in passing bills in both houses of Congress providing the Territory with more protection from the Indians and an improved mail service. Therefore, said Lobato, it was not only "right and just," but politically expedient to retain the Slave Code. The only reason one had not been passed sooner, he suggested, was the scarcity of slaves in the Territory.[56] Under Otero's influence the legislature reluctantly allowed the repeal bill to die in Committee.[57] Immediately after the outbreak of the Civil War in 1861, however, it was repealed.

The issue of slavery expansion was debated in New Mexico, and as was the case in Washington, it was related to the environment of the territory. Thus in Congress Daniel Webster and John Bell insisted that the climate and soil of New Mexico would not support the institution of slavery.[58] They felt that the lack of rain and arid soil made it impossible to conceive of Southerners transporting valuable slaves to a region so unsuited for raising crops. On the other hand, William H. Seward, and others, thought that slaves might be profitably employed in New Mexican industrial and mining activities.

The question was discussed by political figures at the territorial level. W. W. H. Davis, following his return to Pennsylvania from his five-year stay in New Mexico, made this observation:

> In spite of the fears of the abolitionists . . . there is every probability to New Mexico becoming a free state. The whole matter has been more wisely regulated by nature than can be ordered by man. The greater portion of the country is not adapted to slave labor, which would be found too unprofitable to warrant its introduction. The main branch of agriculture which the Territory at present supports . . . is grazing . . . the climate is too cold for . . . crops that would yield a profitable return to Slave Labor. A greater barrier than climate is the cheapness of peon labor, which is less expensive to the proprietor . . . a person can perform as much work and can be hired what it will cost to clothe and feed a negro, with the further advantage of the master having no capital invested in him, which he must lose at the death of the slave.[59]

An Army officer stationed in New Mexico agreed with Davis:

The profits of labor are too inadequate for the existance [sic] of negro slavery. Slavery, as practiced by the Mexicans, under the form of peonage has all the advantages. It enables a master to receive the services of an adult until he is in the prime of life without the obligations of rearing him in his infancy, supporting him in his old age, and maintaining his family.[60]

Also agreeing was Governor Rencher:

In this Territory, there is no excitement upon other questions which are now distracting other portions of the Union. In all the popular meetings which I have noticed, the people express great attachment to the Union, an ernest desire that it may be preserved. In this Territory there is not perhaps more than two dozen slaves, and these are here only temporarily in the Service of public officers. It can never be otherwise in New Mexico, and no efforts on the part of designing men can ever disturb the public by agitating the question of slavery.[61]

Lieutenant Henry M. Lazelle, after conducting a careful geographic survey, concluded that while tobacco, cotton, sugar, and rice might be grown in some areas, "the stables of Southern labor which the climate of New Mexico is capable of supporting . . . are few in number and limited to the boundaries compounding insignificant in extent."[62]

Few insiders, if any, differed from these views, which suggests that Webster and Bell were correct and Seward was wrong. Before accepting this conclusion, however, one must consider the vast size of the territory and its variety of climatic conditions—a fact overlooked by the Webster-Bell group. In the Lower Pecos Valley, for example, cotton is today a very profitable crop and might well have been grown in the nineteenth century with the utilization of slaves, for then there were no peons located in that unsettled area. In fact, the editor of the *Santa Fe Republican* maintained in 1848 that the vast area of New Mexico would attract people from every section of the nation. The resources and commercial advantages of the territory, he predicted, "will cause it in no very distant day, to be thronged with it's [sic] millions, who activated by the restless and indomitable enterprise of race, will cast their lot in the new land that will be opened to them. Among these, Slaveholders, from the fact, that it is nearest and best known to a slave holding population."[63]

Moreover, the mining industry, as subsequent events would prove, required masses of cheap labor and would have to import thousands of European, Asian, and Mexican workers.[64] Had slavery not been destroyed by the Civil War, it is quite possible that blacks would have been used in the mining industry in southwestern New Mexico and southern Colorado as they were employed in the Tredeger Iron Works in Richmond. Even if slave labor had not proved profitable, slavery might still have expanded into New Mexico because of its proximity to the South.[65] As it turned out, however, the most serious slave problem in New Mexico did not involve blacks, numbering but one hundred in 1861, but rather Indian slaves who numbered in the thousands.[66]

Internal Improvements

In his first message to the legislature, James S. Calhoun urged the necessity of caution in selecting the capitol, as the buildings which housed the government at Santa Fe were in bad state of disrepair. "There is not a room in it [the Palace of the Governors] that does not require repairs."[67] To make matters worse the army refused to leave the portion of the building it occupied, insisting the structure had been originally designed to provide quarters for the military commander. Calhoun had to protest to the federal government to force the army to evacuate the building.[68]

There was also present in New Mexico a critical need for jails and a penitentiary, for as Calhoun suggested, "a ten penny nail will let any fellow out of any jail in the country."[69] Indeed, conditions were so bad that the following shocking incident was reported in 1852:

> Phillip Garcia, arrested and convicted for two petty offenses, was chained to the leg of another prisoner in the hope that both would be retained. They did not get along and eventually had a violent quarrel that ended only after Garcia

killed his cell mate. He then cut off the leg of the corpse and
was in the act of escaping when discovered. He was stopped,
tried for murder, found guilty, executed on 29th May, 1852.[70]

In 1853 Congress responded to the need for repair and construction of government offices and penal institutions by appro-
priating $20,000 for construction of a new capitol. A year later
the sum was increased to $70,000 with $20,000 being added for
erection of a penitentiary.[71] Construction of the penitentiary, however, was not commenced until 1855, the work delayed because
its location became the subject of a controversy between Governor Meriwether and the legislature. Four legislators protested the
chosen site because they thought it too close to the homes of resi-
dents and insisted that it be changed to one they selected. The complaint was forwarded to Washington but was rejected by a committee of Congress which declared that only Congress could change
the site. The committee then accepted one chosen by Meriwether.
Construction was eventually begun, with Anglo merchants such as
Ceran St. Vrain, Joab Houghton, and Theodore Wheaton realizing
huge financial gains from materials they sold the government.[72]

The erection of the building proceeded slowly because of a
shortage of bricklayers. Hoping to speed the work, Meriwether
tried to induce bricklayers to come to Santa Fe from the States. He
was shocked when they refused to do so unless they were guaranteed a wage of $12.50 per thousand for making and laying bricks,
which was seven dollars above the average price. Consequently,
he urged Joab Houghton, the chairman of the commission administering the construction of the penitentiary, to use stones or adobe
rather than bricks. Actually, Houghton, who controlled the stone
quarries, had already decided to use stones, giving as his reason
that adobe would "melt" in an expected heavy rainy spell.[73] The
secretary of the treasury, James Guthrie, although astonished at
Houghton's remarks, nevertheless reluctantly approved the use of
stones.[74] Houghton realized great profit not only from the sale of
stone, but from lime and other materials as well.

Although Mexican-American prisoners were employed as
common laborers, and thus were paid little or nothing for their
work, the price of skilled labor increased to the point where Meri-

wether declared a "wage freeze" with the following ceiling prices:

One Master, Carpenter, and Draftsman $4.00 per day	
Two Carpenters:	
one at	3.00 per day
one at	2.50 per day
One Master Mason	3.50 per day
Five Masons	3.00 per day
Five Masons	2.50 per day
Three Overseers	2.50 per day
One Teamster	1.50 per day
Machinist to handle Derricks	3.00 per day
Quarriers (sufficient number)	1.50 per day
Common Laborers	1.00 per day

He further stipulated: "Each master mechanic must certify that mechanics employed under him are of the class described and for which they'd been employed. Overseers and master mechanics must also hand in by two o'clock each day a list of employees and the number of days work since last paid."[75] Houghton protested that the wage restrictions would result in the loss of some of his most skilled help, including his master mason. In fact, he observed, he needed more overseers.[76]

In the end, the money was expended before the end of 1856, but neither the capitol nor the penitentiary was completed. Congress was immediately besieged with requests for more money to complete the capitol and build a larger penitentiary. This money was not granted until 1859 when parts of the penitentiary walls had crumbled and many repairs had to be made on the already completed sections of the capitol. Whatever hopes were present that the projects would ever be finished ended with the outbreak of the Civil War; during the conflict the penitentiary fell into a state of ruin, and the building designed to be the capitol was eventually used as a federal building when completed in the postwar period.

The Palace of the Governors had so badly deteriorated by 1858 that Governor Abraham Rencher, realizing that the new capitol might not be completed, begged the U.S. Secretary of State, Lewis Cass, to provide him funds to make repairs on the old structure. He stated that the building contained offices for the governor, military commander, secretary of the territory, superintendent of Indian affairs, as well as the legislative chambers, a library, post office, and finally, an arms room.[77] Cass provided some emergency funds, but it was not until 1859 that enough money was appropriated by Congress to make the repairs that made the building habitable and ensured its preservation as a treasure of the past.[78]

The territorial officials were more successful in soliciting funds for improving the postal service from Independence to Santa Fe. Governor Rencher was so pleased with the efficiency of the mail service in 1858 that he declared it to be

> not only a blessing to the civilized, but they are the civilizer of the Savage; and nothing can contribute more to tame and subdue the wild Indian and add safety to travel across the plains, than the frequent and certain transmission of the Mail Stage. But we may not hail these mail facilities not only as a present good, but as a harbinger of a future and still greater improvement, confident that the crack of the coach whip is to be followed, at no distant day, by the shrill and animating whistle of the steam engine.[79]

Under the direction of Captain John N. Macomb, roads were also considerably improved. So thorough was his work that Rencher commended Macomb in 1859 for building the routes of communication that served both the military and commercial needs of the territory.[80]

The Mexican-Americans as Politicians

Introduction

Mexican-Americans in the United States total 6.3 million people. In states such as California (16 percent), Colorado (13 percent), Texas (18 percent), and Arizona (19 percent), they form sizeable minorities and must be reckoned with at the polls by aspiring politicians. The political fact that makes New Mexico different, however, is that in this state Mexican-Americans are 40 percent of the population today. Consequently, unlike the other states, they are able to display their political clout in New Mexico to the point where they are powerful enough to share important offices with the Anglos and help shape and mold policies on both state and national levels. The names of Dennis Chavez, Antonio M. Fernandez, Manuel Lujan, and Joseph M. Montoya have accompanied Anglo ones on the roster of New Mexican senators and representatives in Washington. It is only in the governorship that Anglos have been dominant. However, as noted earlier, in 1974 a Mexican-American, Jerry Apodaca, was elected as chief executive of the state.

Moreover, in the first days of the Anglo occupation the Mexican-Americans formed an overwhelming *majority* of the voters who in turn were generally controlled by richer Hispanos. Consequently, while they could not control the executive branch (the governor was appointed by the president), Hispanos could dominate the legislature. And it is interesting to note how they almost immediately realized that their political power could be utilized to prevent complete Anglo domination. On occasion some would complain that they could not understand the new Anglo concept of the law, and should be granted a period to learn the new system of political concepts and values. The majority, however, were able to respond to the new political challenge at both territorial and federal levels. And this response is more deserving of respect when one realizes that although historians of the South have reiterated that their region was the only part of the United States to suffer conquest and occupation by a foreign army along with the hardships and humiliation that accompany defeat in war, New Mexico also was subjected to military defeat and occupation. Other historians have suggested that this military rule lasted only from 1846 to 1851. If one reads carefully into the history of the 1850s, however, one discovers that New Mexicans were subjected to the whims and caprices of the military until the Civil War. Moreover, tensions were heightened by the fact that those who formed the army of occupation were of a different ethnic origin and, as a result of feelings of superiority, were cavalier in their treatment of the "natives." These factors make the achievement of the Mexican-Americans even more important in that, despite the obstacles, they were able to react in positive fashion when it came to filling the roles as representatives of their people in the state legislature as well as acting as delegates to the House of Representatives in Washington.

The Legislature

Under the Organic Law of 1850 legislative power in New Mexico was entrusted to a bicameral body consisting of a House numbering twenty-three members and a Council of thirteen. Annual sessions of forty days were stipulated in the law, but later the length of each session was increased to sixty days. The federal government paid the salaries and mileage allowances of the members. The legislature was empowered to debate and pass bills, and the governor to veto bills. Congress, of course, had to approve all legislation.[1]

The vast majority of legislators in both the House and Council were Mexican-Americans; in 1851, for example, of the ninety-one candidates seeking election to office, all but fourteen were Mexican-American, and in the 1855/1856 session there was but one Anglo seated in the House. In addition, the office of Delegate to Congress was elective, and during all but two years, was occupied by a Mexican-American. Control of these offices gave the Mexican-Americans an influence that afforded them some political protection against the Anglo invaders. Most members were unable to speak English, necessitating the publication of the legislative proceedings in both the English and Spanish languages.

Many Anglo observers thought that the Mexican-Americans were incompetent. W. W. H. Davis felt that this was true because they had no experience in self-government:

> For many years General Manuel Armijo governed New Mexico pretty much in accordance with his own individual predilections; he was the legislative as well as the executive— the judge and the jury in all cases whatsoever and united the whole government within himself.[2]

Davis was generalizing on his personal experiences and obviously had not studied the historical evidence. For, as Lansing Bloom has noted, there was present in New Mexico a Spanish tradition of representation that dated back to the Roman municipium and was perpetuated through the Cortes and the Congress in Mexico City, in addition to the ayuntamiento on the municipal level. After Mexico achieved independence in 1822, provincial legislative bodies were erected which continued to hold sessions until the coming of the Anglo-American in 1846. "No one," says Bloom, "can read the minutes of its sessions during this twenty-five years without realizing that its deliberations and legislative enactments affected every line of common weal."[3]

The opening of New Mexico's first legislative session under the Kearny Code, in 1848, drew the following reluctant accolade from an Anglo reporter:

> I have had a sight of the Territorial Legislature, and I am

really disappointed in finding so intelligent looking an assembly of Mexicans. I am certain they are not just representatives
of their constituents, for a more ignorant and degraded lot
never set up pretensions to civilization than a large majority
of the population of this Territory. It is gratifying to the
friends of the republican form of government to see the
foundation being laid here for such a one; and although the
administration of Civil government consists more in form
than in reality, yet it is both pleasing and instructive to go
through the motions.[4]

The impression conveyed, in a disdainful fashion, is that the
legislators were much better prepared to assume their duties than
has been suggested by Davis and other Anglo historians. After the
legislature was organized with quick dispatch, the same observer
noted:

Proceedings in both houses conducted in dignity and de-
corum and in a manner highly creditable to men unaccus-
tomed to any system of legislature. All that is wanted is a little
time and a little labor to make New Mexico a worthy and
respectable portion of the United States. I am highly gratified
of the industry of members and desire to ameliorate conditions
among the people.[5]

In fact, the only awkward moment of the session occurred when
one of the legislators sent word that he was unable to attend the
first week's meetings because he had been mistaken for the insur-
gent Manuel Cortez and arrested en route to the session.[6]

Things moved smoothly in the first session until the Anglo-
Americans insisted that the legislature pass a law allowing judges
and justices of the peace the authority to join persons in marriage.
Such a proposition was so repugnant to the Mexican-Americans
that all but one of the Council members disapproved of the bill,
and that body adjourned rather than debate the matter. The House
was left to decide what course of action it should now take, since
there was no provision in the Kearny Code dealing with the matter
of one House arbitrarily adjourning itself.[7]

Despite this impasse, and the interference from the military
commanders, the pre-territorial legislatures continued to operate,

passing new laws and reaffirming old laws from the Spanish and
Mexican periods. Included in the legislation passed were acts dealing with the election of alcaldes and constables; cemetery sites;
salaries and emoluments for sheriffs and clerks of court; definitions
of crimes and punishments; grounds for divorce (defined as bar-
barous treatment and making life intolerable); rights of widows;
the introduction of usage of common law in all cases not consistent
with statutory law; conduct and duties of county prefects; conduct
of merchants; and the necessity for county audits.[8] The legislature
attempted to pass a land registry law but failed because of the opposition of General Price and the negative attitude of the military
authorities.

When Calhoun assumed the governorship in 1851, however,
he immediately ordered an election of officers for the legislature.
The ratio of councilors was one per 4,324 inhabitants, and one per
2,192 inhabitants for members of the House. Districts having the
largest surpluses of population were entitled to have extra councilors and representatives.[9] The elections in 1851 were adjudged
to be both corrupt and violent by Anglo-American observers. At
Anton Chico, unregistered soldiers and teamsters voted "three and
four times."[10] In Bernalillo County three men were killed and several wounded, and at Los Ranchos a conflict occurred between
Mexican-Americans and Anglos that resulted in a pitched battle in
which two outsiders were killed.[11] These conflicts exacerbated
the angers between the Anglos and Mexican-Americans.[12]

Nevertheless, the legislature met in June and commenced its
work with great enthusiasm. The members debated and passed
forty-three acts, resolutions, and memorials that included loans
and pay for members and officials; the conduct of a census; contracts for public printing; the organization of judicial districts, and
the territorial militia; relations between masters and servants; maintenance of the acequias; the rights of the people; regulation of
elections correcting the more obvious abuses; and the incorporation
of the city of Santa Fe. Moreover, the governor was authorized to
make a loan of $10,000 to help meet the costs of government until
the arrival of the appointed secretary for the Territory, and finally,
Congress was "memorialized" to conduct a geological survey.[13]

No land or property tax bills were considered by the legislature as the members could not comprehend such a need, having

subsisted before the occupation on the imposts made on the Missouri traders. In the coming decade they remained adamant against a land tax and supported the government by approving only bills that forced the Missouri merchants to pay high license fees and taxes on sales in their stores.

The issue of property taxes was a continuing controversy between the governor and the legislature. Calhoun, Lane, Meriwether, and Rencher all failed in their attempts to have laws passed levying taxes on land. Rencher, faced with mounting debts and no income in 1857, warned that the entire government would be on the verge of collapse if the legislature failed to provide money. His pleas fell on deaf ears[14] as the only new taxes levied were once again on the merchants who complained anew of the burden being imposed on them.[15] Rencher and the other Anglos failed to realize that land taxes were contrary to New Mexican tradition. Moreover, the Mexican-Americans believed that Anglo-Americans, having seized the territory, should pay for its upkeep. Collins, the politically ambitious Superintendent of Indian Affairs and editor of the local newspaper, recognized this attitude and was unwilling to support the unpopular cause of tax reform.[16]

The need for a new apportionment of seats cropped up in 1859 as a result of some population shifts. For example, Santa Fe and Valencia counties had equal populations by 1856, and yet Santa Fe had four members in the legislature while Valencia had but three.[17] The situation was corrected in the 1860 session when a more equal plan of representation was accepted by the legislature.

To some Anglos the largely Mexican-American legislature made amazing progress in developing legislative skills between 1846 and 1861. There were few instances of corruption (although in the 1855 session some members collected full pay, despite the fact they left the assembly early), and Rencher in his 1857 message noted that in comparison to Kansas, the legislature of New Mexico behaved quite well. He suggested that the wisdom of the legislature made it possible for the territory to grow free of "foreign factions as border ruffians."[18] Some Anglo observers, however, continued to be critical:

The legislature will adjourn on the 4th proximo—It is

said to be the weakest and most inefficient body of its kind ever assembled in the Territory, if not in the world. Their labors have been no doubt sufficiently arduous, but so far wholly fruitless for good. About the first thing they did was to whitewash Pelham, the Surveyor General and recommended him for confirmation to the Senate as a "party measure," notwithstanding the facts of him having seduced the girl, and of his living with her in concubinage were notorious, and well known to them.[19]

Another Anglo observer made similar comments after reviewing the actions of the legislature: "You have never seen a more perfect set of J. A. as our present legislature. No preceding legislative body of our territory has been troubling more upon the *Principles of Justice* and endeavors to sacrifice every person who permits not to be used as a tool of the majority and conform to the so called Dem. principles."[20]

Some Anglos felt that as long as the Mexican-Americans dominated the legislature, it would remain degraded. Thus one Missourian suggested in 1855 that it would be the greatest blessing in the world for the territory if legislative powers were taken from the people and given to the general government which would appoint honest men.[21] On the other hand, J. L. Colins noted in 1860: "It is a source of congratulations that the legislature in New Mexico has followed the Constitutional path. Has kept the territory out of the turmoil plaguing Kansas that would be a blow to prosperity and interests. Nothing so conclusive to the welfare of a territory as wholesome legislation."[22] By comparison with the behavior of Anglos and other territorial legislatures in such places as Oregon[23] and Kansas, the Mexican-Americans in New Mexico performed in a creditable fashion despite the Anglo critics.

Delegates to Congress

R. H. Weightman, 1851/1853
Jose Manuel Gallegos, 1853/1855
Miguel Otero, 1855/1861

Although delegates and even "U. S. Senators" had been

elected to Congress in the chaotic period between 1846 and 1851, none had been allowed to take his seat. It was only after the organization of the territory that the delegates were accepted and New Mexico was represented in Congress.

The first delegate was Richard H. Weightman, a Missourian who had raised a battery of artillery as part of Kearny's Army of the West. He had distinguished himself in the Battle of Sacramento "as one of the most gallant figures," and his exploits were well publicized.[24] Following the Mexican War he obtained a position as Indian agent and became actively involved in politics as a supporter of James S. Calhoun and the group attempting to have New Mexico admitted to the Union as a state. In fact, he was elected "U. S. Senator" by the State Party forces in their abortive effort to have New Mexico admitted to the Union in 1850. As was the case with Calhoun, Weightman was popular with the Mexican-Americans because of his efforts to preserve their cultural identity and his support of them against the incursions of the Anglos. He also realized they formed the quantitative base of support necessary for election to any office in New Mexico.

Consequently, in 1851, Weightman, after carefully courting native support, ran for the position of delegate against Captain A. W. Reynolds, the candidate supported by Colonel E. V. Sumner. Despite the pressures exerted by Sumner and the army, Weightman defeated Reynolds by a vote of 4,200 to 3,458.[25] Unfortunately for Weightman and the Mexican-Americans, Reynolds, supported by Missouri Congressmen, contested the election, causing a series of interminable debates in the House that prevented Weightman from being seated until near the end of his term.[26]

Thus little was done on behalf of the Mexican-Americans during Weightman's term, although he did argue for internal improvements, more patronage and appropriations, and better defense against the Indians. In addition, Weightman defended the Mexican-Americans against charges of violence at recent elections, insisting instead that violence at public functions was a rarity until the Anglos intervened.[27] He returned to New Mexico too late to campaign actively for office, but opened a newspaper and remained active in politics until he was forced to leave the territory. After killing Francis X. Aubry, Weightman returned to Missouri and was mortally wounded at the Battle of Wilson's Creek in the first months of the Civil War while serving as a colonel with Sterling Price's forces.

The individual who replaced Weightman in Congress was Jose Manuel Gallegos, a Mexican-American priest who had recently been unfrocked by Bishop Lamy as part of a campaign to replace Mexican clerics with outside priests. Gallegos was supported by Weightman and managed to defeat William Carr Lane for the office of delegate.[28] Lane really had little chance against the Mexican-American in the election, nor was he successful in contesting the results as Thomas Hart Benton, who cordially disliked Lane, threw his weight in Congress against the ex-mayor of St. Louis.[29] The victory of Gallegos was unfortunate for New Mexico as he could not speak a word of English. Consequently, he was most ineffective as a delegate. Gallegos continued, however, to command the loyalty of the Mexican-American clergy.

The most important of the delegates sent to Congress from New Mexico was Miguel Otero, who won over Gallegos in the election of 1855 and dominated New Mexican politics until 1861. Dynamic, intelligent, and very much on the political make, Otero was familiar with the ways of the Anglo, having been educated in St. Louis during his formative years. During his campaign against Gallegos, he employed every means at his disposal to achieve victory, and was ably assisted by his Anglo friends. For example, Elias T. Clark, assigned the task of conveying the poll books from Rio Arriba to Santa Fe, was accosted by Oliver P. Hovey, James Owens, Francis Redman, and William Rowan, all supporters of Otero, who forced him to surrender to them the books which gave the victory to Gallegos. They justified this action with the claim that the Valencia County books which showed Otero the winner in those precincts, had been stolen by the supporters of Gallegos.[30] In the final tally, Gallegos had 8,914 votes to 8,815[31] for Otero, which caused Bishop Lamy to lament, "The party of Padre Gallegos succeeded again and sent him to Congress."[32] It turned out, however, that the House, after conducting an investigation, awarded the seat to Otero.

The new delegate promptly won renown by opposing army operations in New Mexico and advocating a more vigorous policy against the Indians. He was also a staunch supporter of internal improvements, and above all, a fervent propagandist for the erection of a transcontinental railroad through New Mexico. In pursuing this end he became personally acquainted with Jefferson Davis and other Southern leaders and worked closely with them. He cemented his alliance with the Southerners by marrying a girl from South Carolina, but in so doing, provided his political enemies with ammunition to be used against him, as it was charged that his Anglo wife was inclined to look with disdain on Mexican-Americans during her rare visits to the territory. Notwithstanding this handicap, Otero achieved a smashing victory for delegate over his opponent Spruce W. Baird, the ex-Texas judge, in the 1857 election, winning by a vote of 8,498 to 5,986, despite the support Baird received from Gallegos.[33]

Samuel Ellison, a perceptive Anglo politician, provided the following reasons for Baird's defeat: his unpopularity among Mexican-Americans who remembered he once represented the government of Texas; Otero's impressive performance in Congress; Bishop Lamy's opposition to Gallegos; and the support Otero received from Pelham, the surveyor general, whom many Mexican-Americans were hoping would validate their claims. Most important, Otero was a *"Hijo del Pais"* (a son of the country).[34]

During the years from 1857 to 1861, Otero was partially successful in achieving support for some of his internal improvement programs. The Butterfield Overland Mail that ran through New Mexico was subsidized by an annual grant of $600,000 by the federal government, and funds were allotted for construction of a road from Fort Smith, Arkansas, to the Colorado River, through New Mexico Territory. In addition to internal improvements, Otero managed to have the territory declared a land district, making it possible for an office of land registration to be opened, and frustrated the attempts of the Arizonians to form a separate territory.[35] In 1859, following a prior failure, he managed to have Congress appropriate sufficient funds to support both a geological survey and resumption of work on the capitol. Finally, Otero arranged to have a further $75,000 pumped into the office of the Superintendent of Indian Affairs.[36]

The delegate, however, remained most interested in the construction of a transcontinental railroad through the territory and contrived to have the New Mexico legislature pass a bill chartering

the Southern Pacific Railroad in 1859 as a means of winning support in Congress. He further assured such support by inducing the
legislature to pass a slave code for the territory. In return, the
Southerners, led by Jefferson Davis, who desired the same railway
route for their own benefit, supported Otero's proposal for a
southern route.

In the midst of the debates on the railroad, Otero once again
ran for delegate and managed to defeat Gallegos in the ex-priest's
last bid for the office. His days of influence were numbered, however, for within a year Lincoln was elected president and the nation
was confronted with the secession crisis. Otero, disheartened by
events spelling doom for his enterprises, described the Congressional session of 1860:

> From the period of the organization of the House, in
> February last, to it's [sic] adjournment, in June, Congress was
> only in session a little more than four months, and a portion
> of even that time was occupied in doing literally nothing of
> practical legislation for the country generally. The reason of
> course for this abandonment of public interests may be justly
> assigned to the fact that the attention of the members was
> drawn to their party National Conventions, which convened
> during the session of the National Legislature, to nominate
> their respective candidates for the presidency. . . . Thus the
> business of the country was almost wholly neglected.[37]

He managed, however, to receive sufficient funds to pay the militia
for their services in 1855, and the salary for an additional Indian
agent. Moreover, certain private land claims were confirmed
through his efforts.

The outbreak of the Civil War ended Otero's political career.
As a pro-Southerner, he was persona non grata to Lincoln and the
Republicans, and in 1861 was replaced as delegate by John V.
Watts, a strong supporter of the Union. Otero talked vaguely of a
Pacific Confederacy which would include New Mexico along with
other southwestern territories and Pacific states. The confederation
would align with neither the North nor the South. He received little
support for this proposal from his Mexican-American followers.
This was one road on which they would not follow him.

Epilogue

New Mexico on the Eve of the Civil War

Shortly before the presidential election in 1860, the manager of the Exchange Hotel in Santa Fe took a straw ballot among the Anglos who frequented the lobby and announced the following results:

> John C. Breckinridge 55
> Stephen A. Douglas 43
> John Bell 14
> Abraham Lincoln 8

Although it revealed an attitude against the Republican forces of Lincoln, the sampling was probably representative of Anglo opinion in the territory, with the pro-Union sentiment manifested in the votes for Douglas, Bell, and Lincoln outnumbering the pro-Southerners who cast their ballots for Breckinridge.[1]

Other evidence indicates that the Mexican-Americans, with the exception of Miguel Otero and the few followers who supported his plan for a Pacific Confederacy, were overwhelmingly in favor of the Union.[2] This expression of loyalty resulted more from a fear and hatred of Texans than from a feeling of attachment to the United States. As one old *Taosano* recalled, "The Union was the lesser of the evils."[3]

Public proclamation of loyalty was made on July 4, 1860, at a celebration held in Taos where people came from as far as sixty miles to toast the nation. There, even the "recalcitrant" Padre Martinez spoke in favor of perpetuating the Union, and Judge Juan Valdez of the Probate Court added his words of support.[4] Furthermore, a number of Mexican-Americans called a convention for the purpose of writing a constitution and seeking admission to the Union as a "free state."[5] By the spring of 1861, according to Samuel Ellison, the masses of Mexican-Americans were determined to resist any Confederate invasion that came from Texas.[6] A reporter for the *Missouri Republican* later observed, "The native population are [sic] at last thoroughly imbued with the belief that the dreaded Texans are really coming and that agreeably [sic] to the Governor's proclamation, they must either fight or run."[7]

Among the Anglos, however, some Confederate sentiment was expressed. W. Claude Jones, a Southerner, addressed a crowd at Tucson on the rights of the Confederacy and called for a resolution of support for the South.[8] At a public meeting in Santa Fe, called to hear a reading of Lincoln's first inaugural address, Southern sympathizers proposed to seize federal property in the town, which was protected by only fifty soldiers. The plan was rejected, although a reporter present thought it might have succeeded. He wrote that "Seven-eighths of the *Army officers* and citizens, able to think, in New Mexico, are guilty of disloyalty."[9] Although this estimate of disloyal persons was exaggerated, Unionists were jittery and were reassured only when the commanding officer at Fort Garland assumed a vigorous stance in the face of the Confederate threat.[10]

Some Anglos wished to follow a neutral policy. For example, the editor of the *Santa Fe Weekly Gazette,* in warning the Texans they would be "humiliated" once again if they invaded New Mexico, warned them to stay out of the territory:

> What is the position of New Mexico? The answer is a short one. She desires to be let alone. No interference from one side or the other of the sections that are now waging war. She neither wants abolitionists or secessionists from abroad to mix in her affairs at present; nor will she tolerate either. In her

own good time she will say her say, and choose for herself the position she wishes to occupy in the new disposition of the now disrupted power of the United States.[11]

Others suggested New Mexico follow the lead of Missouri in deciding her political future as so many "Americans" were natives of that state.[12]

Governor Abraham Rencher, a North Carolinian, was convinced that the disloyal soldiers and citizens would not be able to overcome the Unionists. Nevertheless, fearing an invasion from Texas, he raised two regiments of infantry, attempted to muster a regiment of cavalry,[13] and called upon every county to provide a home guard[14] in his efforts to retain New Mexico within the Union.

When Henry Connelly assumed the office of governor in November 1861, he called for two additional volunteer companies of infantry and six companies of cavalry. The overwhelming response caused him to pay tribute to a people so "patriotic in nature."[15] During the war over thirty-five hundred men were recruited for service to the Union cause out of a population of fifty thousand. They played key roles in the victories won both over the Confederates and the Indians whose attacks increased during the Civil War.

The outpouring of patriotism was not so remarkable in view of the hatred Mexican-Americans felt toward Texas. In the end they would regard any Confederate-based invasion of New Mexico as a land-grabbing effort on the part of Texas. Consequently, any feeling of alienation was temporarily buried in the unity of the war but would reappear after the conflict.

Retrospect and Prospect: The Angry Chicano

In 1846, according to young Chicano leaders, a traditional Mexican-American agrarian society possessed of a unique cultural heritage was conquered by the Anglo-Americans. In the years following the occupation the Hispano elitists, who had dominated this paternalistic society, formed a partnership with the Anglos which enabled them to continue exploiting the masses. Pedro Perea, Jose D. Sena, J. Francisco Chaves, and Miguel Otero, among others, joined with such men as Thomas B. Catron, Stephen B. Elkins, and

L. Bradford Prince to form political machines that controlled New
Mexico after the Civil War. One reason the Mexican-Americans did
not break the power of the ruling class was that they did not possess the educational tools enabling them to do so. The elite, for
obvious reasons, was not interested in providing educational opportunities, and the federal government, which might have fur-
nished support, failed to act.[16] This neglect of education, insist
Chicanos, continued until the 1960's. Mexican-American children
were forced to attend schools that were sometimes segregated on a
de facto basis (Las Vegas was an example) or, when allowed to
share school accommodations with Anglos, were many times encouraged to drop out as soon as possible and attend trade schools.
Discriminating education persisted in New Mexico until the year
following World War II when defense workers arriving in great
numbers forced a revision. Many rich Anglos sent their sons to the
New Mexico Military Institute, founded in 1891 at Roswell; many
more fortunate Mexican-Americans sent their sons to St. Michael's
College and their daughters to Loretto Academy; but the children
of the masses of Mexican-Americans were forced to attend poorly
supported parochial and public schools and most of them joined the
population of drop-outs.

According to Chicanos, the Church under Archbishop Lamy,
while it expressed interest in saving souls, paid scant attention to
the educational or material needs of Mexican-Americans. Beautiful
edifices were constructed in the midst of grinding poverty. And in
the clergy, avenues for advancement were closed to Mexican-
Americans, dominated as the Church was by a white French and
Irish clergy who allowed few of the natives to enter its ranks.[17]
Even until recently, those Mexican-Americans who were admitted
to the priesthood or brotherhood were seldom offered the opportunity to attain a high office. Indeed, it was not until 1974 that a
Mexican-American, Archbishop Robert F. Sanchez, was named to
head the Archdiocese of Santa Fe.

The problems of the present are many and serious; some of
them common to all American society, some of them the result of
the impact of an alien culture on a native one. Alcoholism is now
a grave problem. Drug addiction is high, and the diet of poverty-
stricken Mexican-Americans is yet so poor that it causes mental
retardation in many cases. The existence of an ethnic caste system

has resulted in a sense of defeatism among Mexican-Americans.[18] "And yet," Rodolfo "Corky" Gonzales has observed, "the legend persists that the Anglo Conquest was conducive to a better way of life."[19]

The Chicanos will no longer tolerate this situation of inequality. "Society," insists Gonzales, "even when it is trying to be benevolent, is a controlled society within which the Anglo makes all the decisions. . . . As a result, my people have been politically destroyed and economically exploited."[20]

In a questionnaire submitted in 1971-72 to five hundred Mexican American students at the College of Santa Fe and New Mexico Highlands University, a question concerned with inequality was included: In your everyday interaction with the Anglo, how frequently do you feel he regards you as an equal? The responses to this question are as follows:

Always	15.4%	Seldom	14.1%
Usually	26.6%	Never	3.9%
Sometimes	37%	Uncertain	3.0%

Those who noted instances of inequality were then asked to state why they felt the Anglos seldom or never regarded them as equals:

Anglos feel superior—10.9%
Anglos discriminate against Mexican-Americans—3.1%
Language and cultural barriers—0.8%
Anglos feel superior and are inclined to discriminate—1.6%
Anglos are inclined to discriminate and use cultural
    barriers—2.3%
All of the above—81.3%

Far different were the answers when the Chicanos were asked how often they treated the Anglos as equals, as indicated below:

Always	27.9%	Seldom	4.7%
Usually	34.9%	Never	6.1%
Sometimes	26.4%		

Formerly respected figures among the Mexican-Americans

have lost their "image." An example is Archbishop Lamy, immortalized by Willa Cather and the subject of a biography by Paul Horgan. When asked to evaluate the famous church leader, the students responded as follows:

Very favorable	6.1%	Unfavorable	17.6%
Favorable	10.8%	Very unfavorable	13.5%
Undecided	27.7%	Don't know him	24.3%

The consensus of a large number of Chicanos concerning Lamy is best expressed by a comment made by one of those who viewed him as "unfavorable":

A typical "colonial lord." Upper classman who looked down on lower classmen (most New Mexicans). A racist who surrounded himself by a French clergy, and did away with all Native born New Mexican priests.

Manuel Armijo, the Mexican governor immediately before the occupation, has been all but forgotten by the Chicanos or remembered as a villain by a few. When asked to evaluate him, the students gave the following responses:

Very favorable	1.4%	Unfavorable	6.9%
Favorable	8.3%	Very unfavorable	7.0%
Undecided	34.7%	Don't know him	41.7%

On the other hand, the younger Mexican-Americans had high praise for Cesar Chavez, Reies Tijerina, and Rodolfo "Corky" Gonzales:

	Reies Tijerina	Cesar Chavez	Rodolfo "Corky" Gonzales
Very favorable	18.4%	36.1%	21.1%
Favorable	44.4%	38.1%	22.2%
Undecided	12.3%	10.3%	23.3%
Unfavorable	10.5%	2.1%	6.7%
Very unfavorable	4.4%	13.4%	4.4%
Don't know him	4.4%	————	20.0%
Right, but uses wrong tactics	6.6%	————	2.3%[21]

in the sometimes overly emotional historical interpretations of the Chicano historians—has in almost every instance made the Anglo solely responsible for the distresses suffered by the Mexican-American. These latter historians have in large measure ignored the roles played by the Hispanos who, for the purpose of self-gain, willingly cooperated with the Anglos in victimizing the mass of Mexican-Americans in New Mexico.

Presently, however, a synthesis is occurring. Cooler heads in La Raza Unida are beginning to recognize that perhaps some of the extreme militants are just as inclined to exploit the situation as the Anglo and Hispano elitists were disposed to do in the past. They are organizing more moderate political movements in places such as Rio Arriba and challenging the power of extremists. I can only hope that this phenomenon is a portent of a future in which the Land of Enchantment will be possessed of the harmonious social environment its beautiful geographic setting deserves.

Notes

Chapter 1
The Land of the Great River

1. Ralph P. Bieber, ed., "Letters of William Carr Lane," *New Mexico Historical Review,* 3 (April, 28), pp. 196-97.

2. F. S. Donnell, "When Texas Owned New Mexico to the Rio Grande," *New Mexico Historical Review,* 8 (April, 1933), p. 66.

3. John W. Caughey, "Early Federal Relations with New Mexico" (unpublished thesis, Univ. of California, 1926), p. 26.

4. *Missouri Republican,* April 29, 1847.

5. Stephen Watts Kearny, "Proclamation of Brigadier General Stephen Watts Kearny to the People of Las Vegas, August 14, 1846," *Governors' Papers* (New Mexico State Records Center and Archives, Santa Fe, N.M.).

6. *Missouri Republican,* April 24, 1847.

7. Ibid., June 23, 1846.

8. *Santa Fe Republican,* July 24, 1848.

9. Ibid., August 1, 1848.

10. W. W. H. Davis, *El Gringo, or New Mexico and Her People* (Santa Fe, N.M.: Rydal Press, 1938), pp. 110-11.

11. *Missouri Republican,* April 24, 1850.

12. Ibid., July 7, 1850.

13. *Congressional Globe,* 31 Cong., 1 Sess., Vol. 21, Pt. 2, 1880-81 (July 15, 1850).

14. P. M. Baldwin, "A Historical Note on the Boundaries of New Mexico," *New Mexico Historical Review,* 1 (April, 1930), p. 121.

15. Ibid., pp. 121-22.

16. *Congressional Globe,* 31 Cong., 1 Sess., Vol. 21, Pt. 1, 945 (May 10, 1850).

17. *New York Tribune,* January 24, 1850.

Chapter 2
The Economic Life of New Mexico

1. Carey McWilliams, *North from Mexico: The Spanish-Speaking People in the United States* (Philadelphia: Lippincott, 1949), p. 51.

2. *Missouri Republican,* July 2, 1846.

3. For the best discussion of the importance of the irrigation canals to certain societies, see Karl Wittfogel, *Oriental Despotism: Hydraulic Society* (New Haven, Conn.: Yale Univ. Press, 1957), passim; Charles H. Lange and Carroll L. Riley, eds., *The Southwestern Journals of Adolph F. Bandelier* (Albuquerque, N.M.: Univ. of New Mexico Press, 1966), passim; Thomas G. Glick, *Irrigation and Society in Medieval Valencia* (Cambridge, Mass.: Belknap Press of Harvard Univ. Press, 1970), passim.

4. *Santa Fe Weekly Gazette,* November 24, 1860.

5. Marc Simmons, "Spanish Irrigation Practices in New Mexico," *New Mexico Historical Review* 47 (April, 1972), pp. 135-36; W. Montgomery Watt, *A History of Islamic Spain* (Chicago: Aldine, 1967), passim; Adolf F. Bandelier, *Final Report of Investigation Among the Indians of the Southwestern United States* (Cambridge, Mass.: J. Wilson and Son, 1890), p. 237.

6. Simmons, "Spanish Irrigation," p. 138.

7. *Missouri Republican,* October 31, 1851.

8. Ibid.

9. Lange and Riley, *Bandelier,* pp. 108-9.

10. *Missouri Republican,* October 31, 1851.

11. W. W. H. Davis, *El Gringo* (Santa Fe, N.M.: Rydal Press, 1938), p. 200.

12. *Missouri Republican,* October 31, 1851.

13. James S. Calhoun, "Message to the Legislature of the Territory of New Mexico," June 2, 1851, New Mexico Territorial Papers, National Archives (Univ. of Northern Iowa, Cedar Falls, Iowa), microfilm, roll 1.

14. Daniel Tyler, "New Mexico in the 1820's: The First Administration of Manuel Armijo" (unpublished dissertation, Univ. of New Mexico, 1970), pp. 46-47.

15. Charles Bent to Manuel Alvarez, April 14, 1846, Benjamin M.

Read Collection (New Mexico State Records Center and Archives, Santa Fe, N.M.).

16. D. V. Whiting, Journal, May 13, 1851, New Mexico Territorial Papers, microfilm, roll 1.

17. John Greiner to Luke Lea, April 30, 1852, Annie Heloise Abel, ed., *The Official Correspondence of James S. Calhoun While Indian Agent at Santa Fe and Superintendent of Indian Affairs in New Mexico* (Washington, D.C.: GPO, 1915), p. 530.

18. *The New Mexican,* June 12, 1870.

19. Calhoun, "Message to the Legislature," June 2, 1851.

20. Abraham Rencher to Lewis Cass, October 15, 1860, New Mexico Territorial Papers, microfilm, roll 1.

21. Abraham Rencher to William H. Seward, May 18, 1861, New Mexico Territorial Papers, microfilm, roll 1.

22. *Missouri Republican,* June 2, 1847.

23. Davis, *El Gringo,* p. 195.

24. *Missouri Republican,* October 31, 1853.

25. *The New Mexican,* March 19, 1870.

26. *Missouri Republican,* October 31, 1851; Davis, *El Gringo,* pp. 201-2.

27. *Missouri Republican,* January 10, 1851.

28. Ibid., September 10, 1846.

29. Abraham Rencher, "Message to the Legislature of the Territory of New Mexico," December 9, 1857, New Mexico Territorial Papers, microfilm, roll 1.

30. *Santa Fe Weekly Gazette,* April 4, 1857.

31. Manuel Alvarez Papers, New Mexico State Archives and Records Center, Santa Fe, N.M., passim.

32. *New Mexican Review,* September 4, 1883.

33. Chris Emmett, *Fort Union and the Winning of the Southwest* (Norman, Okla.: Univ. of Oklahoma Press, 1965), pp. 43-46.

34. Josiah Gregg (ed., David Freeman Hawke), *Commerce of the Prairies* (Indianapolis, Ind.: Bobbs-Merrill, 1970), p. 93.

35. Ibid., p. 54.

36. John Townley, "The New Mexico Mining Company," *New Mexico Historical Review* 46 (January 1971), pp. 58-59.

37. Ibid., p. 63.

38. Ibid.

39. Ibid., pp. 64-65.

40. *Missouri Republican,* January 1, 1847.

41. Ibid., December 18, 1847.

42. Ibid., January 1, 1846.

43. Ibid., January 31, 1849.

44. Ibid., January 28, 1852.

45. Ibid., March 5, 1852.

46. Ibid., December 8, 1851.

47. Ibid., August 24, 1853.

48. *New York Daily Times,* February 2, 1854.

49. Ibid.

50. "Anonymous to W. W. H. Davis," in Robert Helpler, "William Watts Hart Davis in New Mexico" (unpublished thesis, Univ. of New Mexico, 1941), p. 76.

51. *Missouri Republican,* December 18, 1861.

52. Abraham Rencher to Jacob Thompson, Secretary of the Interior, September 10, 1857, Ritch Collection (Univ. of New Mexico, Albuquerque, N.M.), microfilm, roll 4.

53. Helpler, "Davis," p. 189.

54. *Missouri Republican,* October 28, 1851.

55. Gregg, *Commerce of the Prairies,* pp. 61-62.

56. Daniel Tyler, "New Mexico in the 1820's: The First Administration of Manuel Armijo" (unpublished dissertation, Univ. of New Mexico, 1970), p. 46.

57. *Missouri Republican,* October 31, 1851.

58. Ibid.

59. Ibid., January 1, 1847.

60. Anonymous, "Interview with Jose Francisco Chavez," Ritch Collection, microfilm, roll 6.

61. Ibid.

62. Ibid.

63. W. Z. Angney to Manuel Alvarez, November 3, 1852, Manuel Alvarez Papers (New Mexico State Archives and Records Center, Santa Fe, N.M.).

64. Ibid., January 31, 1853.

65. Francis X. Aubrey to Manuel Alvarez, March 15, 1853, Manuel Alvarez Papers.

66. W. Z. Angney to Manuel Alvarez, March 13, 1854, Manuel Alvarez Papers.

67. *Santa Fe Weekly Gazette,* October 9, 1858.

68. S. Houck to Manuel Alvarez, April 28, 1853, Manuel Alvarez Papers.

69. *Santa Fe Republican,* October 2, 1847.

70. Abraham Rencher, "Message," December 9, 1857.

Read Collection (New Mexico State Records Center and Archives, Santa Fe, N.M.).

16. D. V. Whiting, Journal, May 13, 1851, New Mexico Territorial Papers, microfilm, roll 1.

17. John Greiner to Luke Lea, April 30, 1852, Annie Heloise Abel, ed., *The Official Correspondence of James S. Calhoun While Indian Agent at Santa Fe and Superintendent of Indian Affairs in New Mexico* (Washington, D.C.: GPO, 1915), p. 530.

18. *The New Mexican,* June 12, 1870.

19. Calhoun, "Message to the Legislature," June 2, 1851.

20. Abraham Rencher to Lewis Cass, October 15, 1860, New Mexico Territorial Papers, microfilm, roll 1.

21. Abraham Rencher to William H. Seward, May 18, 1861, New Mexico Territorial Papers, microfilm, roll 1.

22. *Missouri Republican,* June 2, 1847.

23. Davis, *El Gringo,* p. 195.

24. *Missouri Republican,* October 31, 1853.

25. *The New Mexican,* March 19, 1870.

26. *Missouri Republican,* October 31, 1851; Davis, *El Gringo,* pp. 201-2.

27. *Missouri Republican,* January 10, 1851.

28. Ibid., September 10, 1846.

29. Abraham Rencher, "Message to the Legislature of the Territory of New Mexico," December 9, 1857, New Mexico Territorial Papers, microfilm, roll 1.

30. *Santa Fe Weekly Gazette,* April 4, 1857.

31. Manuel Alvarez Papers, New Mexico State Archives and Records Center, Santa Fe, N.M., passim.

32. *New Mexican Review,* September 4, 1883.

33. Chris Emmett, *Fort Union and the Winning of the Southwest* (Norman, Okla.: Univ. of Oklahoma Press, 1965), pp. 43-46.

34. Josiah Gregg (ed., David Freeman Hawke), *Commerce of the Prairies* (Indianapolis, Ind.: Bobbs-Merrill, 1970), p. 93.

35. Ibid., p. 54.

36. John Townley, "The New Mexico Mining Company," *New Mexico Historical Review* 46 (January 1971), pp. 58-59.

37. Ibid., p. 63.

38. Ibid.

39. Ibid., pp. 64-65.

40. *Missouri Republican,* January 1, 1847.

41. Ibid., December 18, 1847.

42. Ibid., January 1, 1846.

43. Ibid., January 31, 1849.

44. Ibid., January 28, 1852.

45. Ibid., March 5, 1852.

46. Ibid., December 8, 1851.

47. Ibid., August 24, 1853.

48. *New York Daily Times,* February 2, 1854.

49. Ibid.

50. "Anonymous to W. W. H. Davis," in Robert Helpler, "William Watts Hart Davis in New Mexico" (unpublished thesis, Univ. of New Mexico, 1941), p. 76.

51. *Missouri Republican,* December 18, 1861.

52. Abraham Rencher to Jacob Thompson, Secretary of the Interior, September 10, 1857, Ritch Collection (Univ. of New Mexico, Albuquerque, N.M.), microfilm, roll 4.

53. Helpler, "Davis," p. 189.

54. *Missouri Republican,* October 28, 1851.

55. Gregg, *Commerce of the Prairies,* pp. 61-62.

56. Daniel Tyler, "New Mexico in the 1820's: The First Administration of Manuel Armijo" (unpublished dissertation, Univ. of New Mexico, 1970), p. 46.

57. *Missouri Republican,* October 31, 1851.

58. Ibid.

59. Ibid., January 1, 1847.

60. Anonymous, "Interview with Jose Francisco Chavez," Ritch Collection, microfilm, roll 6.

61. Ibid.

62. Ibid.

63. W. Z. Angney to Manuel Alvarez, November 3, 1852, Manuel Alvarez Papers (New Mexico State Archives and Records Center, Santa Fe, N.M.).

64. Ibid., January 31, 1853.

65. Francis X. Aubrey to Manuel Alvarez, March 15, 1853, Manuel Alvarez Papers.

66. W. Z. Angney to Manuel Alvarez, March 13, 1854, Manuel Alvarez Papers.

67. *Santa Fe Weekly Gazette,* October 9, 1858.

68. S. Houck to Manuel Alvarez, April 28, 1853, Manuel Alvarez Papers.

69. *Santa Fe Republican,* October 2, 1847.

70. Abraham Rencher, "Message," December 9, 1857.

Chapter 3
The Mexican-Americans—The Insiders Looking Out

1. This opinion is based on many conversations with Mexican-Americans and the conducting of a survey at three universities in New Mexico (Univ. of New Mexico, College of Santa Fe, and New Mexico Highlands Univ.). Very few of those queried, ranging in age from eighteen to thirty-five, are inclined to reject the Indian heritage or, conversely, to accept the term "Hispano."

2. "Census of 1790, Albuquerque Jurisdiction" (New Mexico State Records Center and Archives, Santa Fe, N.M.).

3. "Census Report," April 24, 1851, New Mexico Territorial Papers, National Archives (Univ. of Northern Iowa, Cedar Falls, Iowa), microfilm, roll 1.

4. "Instructions to the Convention of Delegates, 1849," pp. 20-22, New Mexico Territorial Papers, microfilm, roll 1.

5. James S. Calhoun, "Message to the Legislature of the Territory of New Mexico," June 2, 1851, New Mexico Territorial Papers, microfilm, roll 1.

6. *Congressional Globe,* 30 Cong., 1 Sess., Appendix, 1060-61 (July 29, 1848).

7. Ibid., Appendix, 144 (January 31, 1848).

8. Ibid., Appendix, 1072-73 (August 3, 1848).

9. W. W. H. Davis, *El Gringo* (Santa Fe, N.M.: Rydal Press, 1938), pp. 232-33.

10. *Missouri Republican,* October 31, 1851.

11. *Santa Fe Republican,* February 2, 1848, Ritch Collection (Univ. of New Mexico, Albuquerque, N.M.), microfilm, roll 5.

12. "Notes," May 10, 1851, New Mexico Territorial Papers, microfilm, roll 1.

13. Ibid., April 3, 1851.

14. 1st Lt. S. D. Sturgis to Major W. A. Nichols, Ritch Collection, microfilm, roll 4.

15. Lawrence R. Murphy, "Reconstruction in New Mexico," *New Mexico Historical Review,* 43 (April 1968), p. 101.

16. *Missouri Republican,* August 20, 1846.

17. Ibid., October 26, 1846.

18. Ibid., October 13, 1846.

19. Fernando Aragon to Donaciano Vigil, n.d., Vigil Papers (New Mexico State Records Center and Archives, Santa Fe, N.M.), uncatalogued.

20. "Notes," Ritch Collection, microfilm, roll 4.

21. Calhoun, "Message," June 2, 1851.

22. *Missouri Republican,* October 2, 1851.

23. Interview with Jose Naranjo, August 10, 1968, Santa Fe, N.M.

24. Questionnaires distributed among students at New Mexico High-lands Univ., College of Santa Fe, and the Univ. of New Mexico, Fall and Winter, 1971/1972. This research method was employed because the high illiteracy rate of the Mexican-Americans resulted in a paucity of written evidence, which explains why such questions have not been considered in prior historical treatments dealing with the period.

Chapter 4
The Indians

1. Interview with Harpur Vicentito, Aug. 15, 1969, Santa Fe, N.M.

2. James S. Calhoun to Luke Lea, June 30, 1851, *Official Correspondence of James S. Calhoun,* ed. by A. H. Abel (Washington, D.C., GPO, 1915), p. 369.

3. *Missouri Republican,* July 2, 1846.

4. John Greiner to James S. Calhoun, March 25, 1852, *Official Correspondence of James S. Calhoun,* pp. 494-95.

5. Ibid., p. 495.

6. Ibid.

7. Ibid.

8. Ibid.

9. Ibid., pp. 295-96.

10. Ibid., p. 496.

11. Ibid., pp. 496-97.

12. *Missouri Republican,* October 2, 1851.

13. James S. Calhoun, "Message to the Legislative of the Territory of New Mexico," June 2, 1851, New Mexico Territorial Papers, National Archives (Univ. of Northern Iowa, Cedar Falls, Iowa), microfilm, roll 1.

14. James S. Calhoun to Orlando Brown, January 28, 1850, *Official Correspondence of James S. Calhoun,* p. 119.

15. Ibid., pp. 119-20.

16. Ibid., p. 120.

17. D. V. Whiting, "Notes," April 10, 1851, New Mexico Territorial Papers, microfilm, roll 1.

18. According to Myra Ellen Jenkins, who has done considerable work in this area, Mexican-Americans did attempt to trespass on Pueblo lands by reintroducing land grant claims.

19. John Greiner to Luke Lea, April 30, 1852, *Official Correspondence of James S. Calhoun,* p. 531.

20. *Missouri Republican,* July 2, 1851.

21. W. W. H. Davis, "Message to the Legislature of New Mexico," in Robert D. Helpler, "William Watts Hart Davis in New Mexico" (unpublished thesis, Univ. of New Mexico, 1941), pp. 142-43.

22. Abraham Rencher to Lewis Cass, April 10, 1858, New Mexico Territorial Papers, microfilm, roll 1.

23. James S. Calhoun to Daniel Webster, June 30, 1851, *Official Correspondence of James S. Calhoun,* pp. 362-63.

24. D. V. Whiting, "Notes," n.d., New Mexico Territorial Papers, microfilm, roll 1; *Missouri Republican,* July 28, 1851.

25. D. V. Whiting to Luke Lea, July 5, 1851, *Official Correspondence of James S. Calhoun,* pp. 540-41.

26. *Missouri Republican,* August 16, 1852.

27. *Santa Fe Weekly Gazette,* October 9, 1858.

28. Abraham Rencher to Lewis Cass, April 10, 1858, New Mexico Territorial Papers, microfilm, roll 1.

29. *Missouri Republican,* July 2, 1851.

30. The lodge consisted of a family unit in which the number of persons varied from lodge to lodge.

31. *Missouri Republican,* July 2, 1852.

32. Josiah Gregg (ed., David Freeman Hawke), *Commerce of the Prairies* (Indianapolis, Bobbs-Merrill, 1970), p. 93.

33. Ibid., p. 92.

34. *Missouri Republican,* July 2, 1846.

35. Ibid.

36. Interview with Harpur Vincentito, Aug. 15, 1960, Santa Fe, N.M.

37. *Missouri Republican,* July 2, 1846.

38. This is the attitude supported in the recent work by Odie Faulk entitled *Land of Many Frontiers: A History of the American Southwest* (New York: Oxford University Press, 1968), passim.

39. L. R. Bailey, *Indian Slave Trade in the Southwest* (Los Angeles: Westernlore Press, 1966), p. 143. For a contrasting view, see Albert H. Schroeder, ed., *The Changing Ways of the Southwestern Indians* (Albuquerque, N.M.: Univ. of New Mexico Press, 1973), passim.

40. Bailey, *Indian Slave Trade,* passim.

41. "Report of James S. Calhoun on Captives," 1850, Ritch Collection (Univ. of New Mexico, Albuquerque, N.M.), microfilm, roll 5.

42. *Missouri Republican,* March 19, 1846.

43. J. R. Bartlett, *Personal Narrative of Explorations . . . in Texas,*

New Mexico, California, Sonora, and Chihuahua (Chicago: Regnery, 1965), pp. 215-16.

44. *Missouri Republican,* March 9, 1848.

45. William S. Messervy to Jose Maria Chavez, April 1, 1854, New Mexico Territorial Papers, microfilm, roll 1.

46. William S. Messervy, "Proclamation," n.d., New Mexico Territorial Papers, microfilm, roll 1.

47. Arie Poldervaart, "Black Robed Justice in New Mexico, 1846-1912," *New Mexico Historical Review,* 22 (April, 1947), p. 123.

48. *Missouri Republican,* February 24, 1852.

49. Ibid., January 5, 1852.

50. Louis H. Warner, "Conveyance of Property, The Spanish and Mexican Way," *New Mexico Historical Review,* 6 (August, 1931), pp. 358-59.

51. Poldervaart, "Black Robed Justice," p. 123.

52. John Greiner to Luke Lea, April 30, 1852, *Official Correspondence of James S. Calhoun,* pp. 531, 536; see also *Missouri Republican,* March 27, 1852.

53. "Law of 1851 Concerning Captured Property," New Mexico Territorial Papers, microfilm, roll 1.

54. J. R. Bartlett to A. U. Stuart, Secretary of the Interior, February 19, 1852, Superintendency of Indian Affairs, New Mexico Territorial Papers, microfilm, roll 1.

55. Abraham Rencher, "Message to the Legislature," December 6, 1860, New Mexico Territorial Papers, microfilm, roll 1.

56. Baptismal Records, Holy Trinity Parish, Trinidad, Colorado.

57. Interview with Dean C. Mabry, Judge, Third Judicial District of Colorado, Trinidad, Colorado, January 30, 1969.

58. Although authorities such as Myra Ellen Jenkins disagree with this interpretation, the legal evidence in Trinidad, Colorado, is adequate to justify qualified acceptance of the conclusion.

59. Interview with Dean C. Mabry, Judge, Third Judicial District of Colorado, Trinidad, Colorado, January 30, 1969.

Chapter 5
The Santa Fe Trail

1. Carey McWilliams, *North from Mexico: The Spanish-Speaking People of the United States* (New York: Greenwood Press, 1968), pp. 49-50.

2. Max L. Moorhead, "Spanish Transportation in the Southwest, 1540-1846," *New Mexico Historical Review,* 32 (January, 1957), pp. 120-21.

3. Daniel Tyler, "New Mexico in the 1820's: The First Administration of Manuel Armijo" (unpublished dissertation, Univ. of New Mexico, 1970), p. 238.

4. *Missouri Republican,* February 16, 1846.

5. Tyler, "Armijo," p. 238.

6. Manuel Alvarez Papers (New Mexico State Records Center and Archives, Santa Fe, N.M.).

7. Ibid.

8. *Missouri Republican,* May 23, 1851.

9. Frederic A. Culmer, "Marking the Santa Fe Trail," *New Mexico Historical Review,* 9 (January, 1934), pp. 78-79.

10. Ibid., p. 86.

11. Tyler, "Armijo," p. 264.

12. Culmer, "Marking," p. 87.

13. Tyler, "Armijo," p. 279.

14. Ibid., pp. 280-81.

15. Hubert Howe Bancroft, *History of Arizona and New Mexico* (San Francisco: The History Company, 1889), p. 335.

16. Fred S. Perrine, "Military Escorts on the Santa Fe Trail," *New Mexico Historical Review,* 2 (April, 1927), pp. 176-77.

17. *Missouri Republican*, September 13, 1851.

18. Ibid., May 23, 1853.

19. Ibid., September 2, 1846; *New York Daily Tribune,* September 7, 1846.

20. *Santa Fe Republican,* May 15, 1848; see also Walker D. Wyman, "F. X. Aubry: Santa Fe Freighter, Pathfinder and Explorer," *New Mexico Historical Review,* 12 (January, 1932), pp. 1-31.

21. *Missouri Republican,* June 3, 1848.

22. Ibid., September 23, 1848.

23. Ibid., August 22, 1851.

24. Abraham Rencher to Lewis Cass, November 10, 1857, New Mexico Territorial Papers, National Archives (Univ. of Northern Iowa, Cedar Falls, Iowa), microfilm, roll 1.

25. Robert D. Helper, "William Watts Hart Davis in New Mexico" (unpublished thesis, Univ. of New Mexico, 1941), pp. 143-44.

26. *Missouri Republican,* August 20, 1848.

27. Ibid., November 6, 1847.

28. J. L. Collins to Henry Carr Lane, December 10, 1852, Benjamin M. Read Collection (New Mexico State Records Center, Santa Fe, New Mexico).

29. *Missouri Republican,* September 10, 1846.

30. Ibid., April 24, 1850.

31. Ibid., December 13, 1847.

32. Ibid., January 1, 1846.

33. Ibid., February 19, 1847.

34. The best works to consult for further information on the Santa Fe Trail are Max L. Moorhead, *New Mexico's Royal Road: Trade and Travel on the Chihuahua Trail* (Norman, Okla.: Univ. of Oklahoma Press, 1958), and Leo E. Oliva, *Soldiers on the Santa Fe Trail* (Norman, Okla.: Univ. of Oklahoma Press, 1967). There is also an excellent short study published by the National Park Service as well as two older works: R. L. Duffus, *The Santa Fe Trail* (New York: Tudor, 1930) and Stanley Vestal, *The Old Santa Fe Trail* (Boston: Houghton Mifflin, 1939).

Chapter 6
Anglo Reaction to the Physical Environment

1. In return for the Territory, the United States paid $15 million and agreed to assume the claims of U.S. citizens against Mexico amounting to $3.25 million.

2. *Missouri Republican,* June 25, 1846.

3. William Carr Lane to William Glasgow, September 10, 1852, ed. Ralph P. Bieber, "Letters of William Carr Lane, 1852-1854," *New Mexico Historical Review,* 2 (April, 1927), pp. 185-86.

4. *New Mexican Review,* September 26, 1883.

5. *Missouri Republican,* December 18, 1860.

6. Josiah Gregg (ed., David Freeman Hawke), *Commerce of the Prairies* (Indianapolis, Ind.: Bobbs-Merrill, 1970), pp. 46-47.

7. Robert D. Helpler, "William Watts Hart Davis in New Mexico" (unpublished thesis, Univ. of New Mexico, 1941), p. 193-94.

8. *The Santa Fe Republican,* September 10, 1847.

9. Ibid.

10. Ibid.

11. George T. Weathered to Manuel Alvarez, May 20, 1850, Alvarez Papers (New Mexico State Records Center and Archives, Santa Fe, N.M).

12. "Rental Agreement," n.d., Alvarez Papers.

13. Smyth and Shelly to Manuel Alvarez, October 10, 1849, Alvarez Papers.

14. *Missouri Republican,* January 1, 1846.

15. Lansing Bloom, "New Mexico Under Mexican Administration," *Old Santa Fe,* 2 (April, 1915), p. 355.

16. *Missouri Republican,* March 19, 1846.

17. Josiah Gregg, *Commerce,* pp. 43-44.

18. Edwin Morris to Albert Speyer, July 21, 1845, Alvarez Papers.

19. Ralph Emerson Twitchell, *Old Santa Fe* (Chicago: Rio Grande Press, 1963), 229-30.

20. Charles Irving Jones, ed., "William Kronig, New Mexico Pioneer from his Memories of 1849-1860," *New Mexico Historical Review,* 19 (July, 1944), p. 195.

21. H. Gosselin to Manuel Alvarez, March 10, 1853, Alvarez Papers.

22. William A. Keleher, *Turmoil in New Mexico,* 1946-1868 (Santa Fe, N.M.: Rydal Press, 1952), p. 63.

23. *Santa Fe Gazette* quoted in *Missouri Republican,* April 18, 1853.

24. Ibid.

25. Ibid.

26. Ibid., March 8, 1847.

27. *Congressional Globe,* 30 Cong., 2 Sess., Appendix, 557-58 (February 19, 1849).

28. Abraham Rencher to Lewis Cass, September 10, 1859, New Mexico Territorial Papers, National Archives (Univ. of Northern Iowa, Cedar Falls, Iowa), microfilm, roll 1.

29. John S. Phelps, *Visit of Hon. John S. Phelps to . . . New Mexico* (Quincy, Ill.: n.p., 1859), passim.

30. *Missouri Republican,* October 8, 1846.

31. J. L. Collins to Manuel Alvarez, May 19, 1847, Read Collection (New Mexico State Records Center and Archives, Santa Fe, N.M.).

32. *Missouri Republican,* August 12, 1847.

33. Howard Lamar, *The Far Southwest* (New Haven, Conn.: Yale Univ. Press, 1966), p. 95; Averam Bender, *The March of Empire: Frontier Defense in the Southwest, 1848-1860* (Lawrence, Ka.: Univ. of Kansas Press, 1952), p. 170.

34. Lamar, *Far Southwest,* p. 95.

35. *Santa Fe Republican,* May 15, 1848.

36. *Missouri Republican,* October 25, 1851.

37. *Santa Fe Weekly Gazette,* October 9, 1858.

38. *Missouri Republican,* October 28, 1858.

39. No study of the influence of the army in New Mexico is complete

without taking cognizance of the following books: Robert W. Frazer, ed., *Col. George Archibald McCall, New Mexico in 1850: A Military View* (Norman, Okla.: Univ. of Oklahoma Press, 1968); Leo E. Oliva, *Soldiers on the Santa Fe Trail* (Norman, Okla.: Univ. of Oklahoma Press, 1967).

Chapter 7
Anglo Reactions to the Mexican-Americans—
The Outsiders Looking In

1. Carey McWilliams, *North from Mexico: The Spanish-Speaking People of the United States* (New York: Greenwood Press, 1968), p. 99.

2. McWilliams, *North from Mexico,* p. 129; Leonard Pitt, *The Decline of the Californios: A Social History of the Spanish-Speaking Californians, 1846-1890* (Berkeley: Univ. of California Press, 1966), pp. 15-17. Another excellent study of the cultural confrontation is David J. Weber, *Foreigners in their Native Land* (Albuquerque, N.M.: Univ. of New Mexico Press, 1973).

3. A satisfactory discussion of the Santa Fe Ring is contained in Howard R. Lamar, *The Far Southwest, 1846-1912: A Territorial History* (New Haven, Conn.: Yale Univ. Press, 1966), pp. 136-170.

4. *Congressional Globe,* 29th Cong., 2nd Sess., Vol. 2, 369 (February 12, 1847).

5. Nancie L. Gonzalez, *The Spanish-Americans of New Mexico* (Albuquerque, N.M.: Univ. of New Mexico Press, 1967), p. 80.

6. *Santa Fe Republican,* May 15, 1848, Ritch Collection (Univ. of New Mexico, Albuquerque, N.M.), microfilm, roll 5.

7. J. R. Bartlett, *Personal Narrative of Explorations in Texas, New Mexico . . .* I (Chicago: Regnery, 1965), p. 312.

8. "House Executive Document," *Congressional Globe,* 32 Cong., 2 Sess., No. 37 (Vol. 1, Serial 807), pp. 296-316.

9. Chris Emmett, *Fort Union and the Winning of the Southwest* (Norman, Okla.: Univ. of Oklahoma Press, 1965), p. 159.

10. Ibid.

11. Charles Bent to Manuel Alvarez, n.d., Alvarez Papers (New Mexico State Records Center and Archives, Santa Fe, N.M.); Emmett, *Fort Union,* p. 25.

12. Josiah Gregg (ed., David Freeman Hawke), *Commerce of the Prairies* (Indianapolis, Ind.: Bobbs-Merrill, 1970), p. 71.

13. Ibid., pp. 71-72.

14. E. V. Sumner to C. M. Conrad, January 10, 1853, *Congressional Globe,* 32 Cong., 2 Sess., Appendix, p. 104.

15. *Missouri Republican,* April 29, 1847.

16. Ibid., June 2, 1847.

17. Bartlett, *Personal Narrative,* p. 300.

18. "Speech by Kirby Benedict Before New Mexico Historical Society," December 31, 1960, Ritch Collection, microfilm, roll 5.

19. J. L. Collins to Eliza Collins, October 31, 1856, Ritch Collection, microfilm, roll 4.

20. *Missouri Republican,* April 29, 1847.

21. Ibid.

22. "Wilson's Explanation of Mixed Population," Ritch Collection, microfilm, roll 7.

23. *Missouri Republican,* December 24, 1855.

24. Note by Manuel Alvarez, July 28, 1845, Benjamin Read Collection (New Mexico State Records Center and Archives, Santa Fe, N.M.).

25. *Congressional Globe,* 30 Cong., 1 Sess., Vol. 17, 51 (January 4, 1848).

26. *Congressional Globe,* 29 Cong., 2 Sess., Vol. 16, 516 (February 26, 1847).

27. Ibid.

28. W. W. H. Davis, *El Gringo, or New Mexico and Her People* (Santa Fe, N.M.: Rydal Press, 1938), pp. 431-32.

29. *Missouri Republican,* April 1, 1847.

30. *Missouri Republican,* July 2, 1852.

31. Ibid., August 29, 1853.

32. Ibid., January 10, 1851.

33. Ibid., November 28, 1846.

34. Charles Bent to Alexander W. Doniphan, October 9, 1846, New Mexico Territorial Papers, National Archives (University of Northern Iowa, Cedar Falls, Iowa), microfilm, roll 1.

35. *Missouri Republican,* January 1, 1847.

36. Ibid.

37. Ibid.

38. Ibid., November 29, 1847.

39. Ibid., June 14, 1847; *New York Daily Tribune,* June 12, 1847.

40. *Missouri Republican,* November 11, 1847; December 20, 1847.

41. Ibid., December 20, 1847.

42. Ibid., December 30, 1847.

43. Clinton E. Brooks and Frank D. Reeves, eds., "James Augustus Bennett, Forts and Forays . . . a dragoon in New Mexico, 1850-1856,"

New Mexico Historical Review, 22 (January, 1947), pp. 51-97, 140-176.

44. *Missouri Republican,* January 10, 1851.

45. Abraham Rencher to Lewis Cass, December 11, 1857, New Mexico Territorial Papers, microfilm, roll 1.

46. *Missouri Republican,* April 17, 1857.

47. Interviews with Mexican-Americans, 1961-1971; questionnaires distributed among students at New Mexico Highlands Univ., College of Santa Fe, and the Univ. of New Mexico, Fall and Winter, 1971/1972.

Chapter 8
Culture and Economic Problems Following the Anglo Occupation

1. See Howard Lamar, *The Far Southwest* (New Haven, Conn.: Yale Univ. Press, 1966); Robert W. Larson, *New Mexico's Quest for Statehood, 1846-1912* (Albuquerque, N.M.: University of New Mexico Press, 1968); Loomis Morton Ganaway, *New Mexico and the Sectional Controversy* (Albuquerque, N.M.: Univ. of New Mexico Press, 1944).

2. Chris Emmett, *Fort Union and the Winning of the Southwest* (Norman, Okla.: Univ. of Oklahoma Press, 1965), p. 46.

3. "Report to Governor Baca," January 11, 1825, Benjamin M. Read Collection (New Mexico State Records Center and Archives, Santa Fe, N.M.), No. 31.

4. Ibid.

5. "Notes on Education," Ritch Collection (Univ. of New Mexico, Albuquerque, N.M.), microfilm, roll 5.

6. Daniel Tyler, "Armijo" (dissertation, Univ. of New Mexico, 1970), p. 69.

7. *Missouri Republican,* January 11, 1848.

8. *Congressional Globe,* 29 Cong., 2 Sess., Appendix 130 (January 26, 1847).

9. *Santa Fe Republican,* May 15, 1848.

10. James S. Calhoun, "Message to the Legislature of the Territory of New Mexico," June 2, 1851, New Mexico Territorial Papers, National Archives (Univ. of Norman Iowa, Cedar Falls, Iowa), microfilm, roll 1.

11. Ibid.

12. William Taylor, *Cavalier and Yankee* (London, Eng.: W. H. Allen, 1961), passim.

13. W. W. H. Davis, *El Gringo* (Santa Fe, N.M.: Rydal Press, 1938), p. 194.

14. Ibid.

15. *Missouri Republican,* January 20, 1852.

16. Ibid., November 3, 1851.

17. Ibid., January 20, 1852.

18. Ibid.

19. James S. Calhoun, "Official Correspondence," edited by A. H. Abel (Washington, D.C.: Government Printing Office, 1915), p. 494.

20. Samuel Gorman, "Reminiscences," Ritch Collection, microfilm, roll 7.

21. "Note," March 25, 1852, Ritch Collection, microfilm, roll 7.

22. Alvin R. Sunseri, "St. Michael's College," *La Salle Auxiliary,* 39 (Spring, 1960), pp. 24-25.

23. Davis, *El Gringo,* p. 194.

24. David Meriwether, "Message to the Legislative Assembly of New Mexico," December 5, 1853, New Mexico Territorial Papers, microfilm, roll 1.

25. Robert D. Helpler, "William Watts Hart Davis in New Mexico" (unpublished thesis, Univ. of New Mexico, 1941), p. 153.

26. Meriwether, "Message to the Legislative Assembly of New Mexico," December 1, 1856.

27. Davis, *El Gringo,* p. 195.

28. Meriwether, "Message," December 1, 1856.

29. "Education and Learning," New Mexico Territorial Papers, microfilm, roll 1.

30. Abraham Rencher, "Message," December 3, 1857, New Mexico Territorial Papers, microfilm, roll 1.

31. *Santa Fe Weekly Gazette,* October 9, 1958.

32. "An Act for Compulsory Education," January 27, 1860, New Mexico Territorial Papers, microfilm, roll 1.

33. Rencher, "Message," December 6, 1860.

34. Hubert Howe Bancroft, *History of Arizona and New Mexico, 1530-1888* (San Francisco, 1889), p. 643. See also the following excellent books: Robert W. Larson, *New Mexico's Quest for Statehood, 1846-1912* (Albuquerque, N.M.: Univ. of New Mexico Press, 1968), passim; Victor Westphall, *The Public Domain in New Mexico, 1854-1891* (Albuquerque, N.M.: Univ. of New Mexico Press, 1965), passim.

35. John W. Caughey, "Early Federal Relations with New Mexico" (unpublished thesis, Univ. of California, 1922), p. 74.

36. *Missouri Republican,* January 31, 1849.

37. Ibid.

38. Ibid.

39. Calhoun, "Message," June 2, 1851.

40. C. P. Clever to John V. Watts, December 28, 1855, Ritch Collection, microfilm, roll 4.

41. John V. Watts to William Pelham, February 14, 1857, Ritch Collection, microfilm, roll 4.

42. H. S. Fant to John V. Watts, December 27, 1857, Ritch Collection, microfilm, roll 4.

43. Victor Westphall, "The Public Domain in New Mexico," *New Mexico Historical Review,* 33 (January, 1958), pp. 26-29.

44. *New York Herald,* November 28, 1857.

45. *Santa Fe Weekly Gazette,* October 22, 1860.

46. Robert W. Larson, *New Mexico's Quest for Statehood, 1846-1912* (Albuquerque, N.M.: Univ. of New Mexico Press, 1968), p. 19.

47. Calhoun, "Message," June 2, 1851.

48. *Constitution of the State of New Mexico* (1850), Article 1, Section 1.

49. "Legislative Enactments," New Mexico Territorial Papers, microfilm, roll 2.

50. Helpler, "Davis," pp. 167-68.

51. Ibid., pp. 166-67.

52. Interview with Harpur Vincentito, August 9, 1969, Santa Fe, N.M.

53. Helpler, "Davis," pp. 166-67.

54. Ibid., p. 166.

55. Ibid.

56. "Report of the Special Committee of the House of Representatives of the Territory of New Mexico upon the Bill to repeal the Act of February 3, 1859, for the Protection of Property in Slaves," New Mexico Territorial Papers, microfilm, roll 1.

57. Ibid.

58. Larson, *New Mexico's Quest,* p. 17.

59. Davis, *El Gringo,* pp. 107-8.

60. Loomis M. Ganaway, *New Mexico and the Sectional Controversy* (Albuquerque, N.M.: Univ. of New Mexico Press, 1944), p. 122.

61. Abraham Rencher to Lewis Cass, April 14, 1861, New Mexico Territorial Papers, microfilm, roll 1.

62. *Missouri Republican,* June 22, 1860.

63. *Santa Fe Republican,* January 28, 1848.

64. Alvin R. Sunseri, "The Ludlow Massacre: A Study in the Misemployment of the National Guard," *American Chronicle,* 1 (January, 1972), passim.

65. *Missouri Republican,* June 22, 1860.

66. "Statement of Chief Justice Kirby Benedict," Ritch Collection, microfilm, roll 4.

67. Calhoun, "Message," June 2, 1851.

68. Ibid.

69. *Missouri Republican,* January 5, 1852.

70. Ibid., June 26, 1852.

71. Meriwether, "Message," December 5, 1853.

72. "Address to the Governor," March 30, 1855, Ritch Collection, microfilm, roll 4.

73. David Meriwether to James Guthrie, December 17, 1855, Ritch Collection, microfilm, roll 4.

74. James Guthrie to David Meriwether, April 3, 1856, Ritch Collection, microfilm, roll 4.

75. David Meriwether to Joab Houghton, May 11, 1856, Ritch Collection, microfilm, roll 4.

76. Joab Houghton to James Guthrie, May 22, 1856, Ritch Collection, microfilm, roll 4.

77. Abraham Rencher to Lewis Cass, February 12, 1858, Ritch Collection, microfilm, roll 1.

78. Rencher, "Message," December 8, 1858; Letter to House of Representatives, Territory of New Mexico, January 19, 1859, New Mexico Territorial Papers, microfilm, roll 1.

79. Rencher, "Message," December 8, 1858.

80. Ibid. For a thorough discussion of road construction in New Mexico, see W. Turrentine Jackson, *Wagon Roads West* (New Haven, Conn.: Yale Univ. Press, 1965), pp. 107-120.

Chapter 9
The Mexican-Americans as Politicians

1. John W. Caughey, "Early Federal Relations with New Mexico" (unpublished thesis, Univ. of California, 1926), p. 72. Also, it should be noted that for political matters during this period, the following works should be consulted: Howard H. Lamar, *The Far Southwest* (New Haven, Conn.: Yale Univ. Press, 1966) and Robert W. Larson, *New Mexico's Quest for Statehood* (Albuquerque, N.M.: Univ. of New Mexico Press, 1968).

2. W. W. H. Davis, *El Gringo* (Santa Fe, N.M.: Rydal Press, 1938), p. 254.

3. Lansing Bloom, "Beginnings of Representative Government in

New Mexico," reprint from El Palacio (March, 1922) in *New Mexico Historical Review,* 21 (April, 1946), p. 133.

4. *Missouri Republican,* January 11, 1848.

5. Ibid.

6. Ibid., January 18, 1848.

7. Ibid.

8. Donaciano Vigil Papers (New Mexico State Records Center and Archives, Santa Fe, N.M.), uncatalogued.

9. "Proclamation," April 22, 1851, New Mexico Territorial Papers, National Archives (Univ. of Northern Iowa, Cedar Falls, Iowa), microfilm, roll 1.

10. D. V. Whiting, "Note," New Mexico Territorial Papers, microfilm, roll 1.

11. *Missouri Republican,* November 6, 1851.

12. Ibid., passim.

13. "List of Acts, Resolutions, and Memorials of the Legislative Assembly of the Territory of New Mexico passed at a session begun and held on the Second day of June, 1851," New Mexico Territorial Papers, microfilm, roll 1.

14. Abraham Rencher, "Message to the Legislative Assembly of the Territory of New Mexico," November 15, 1857, New Mexico Territorial Papers, microfilm, roll 1.

15. Robert D. Helpler, "William Watts Hart Davis in New Mexico" (unpublished thesis, Univ. of New Mexico, 1941), p. 148. *Missouri Republican,* September 1, 1851.

16. Abraham Rencher to Lewis Cass, April 10, 1858, New Mexico Territorial Papers, microfilm, roll 4.

17. Helpler, "Davis," pp. 145-46.

18. Rencher, "Message," December 9, 1857, New Mexico Territorial Papers, microfilm, roll 1.

19. Helpler, "Davis," p. 169.

20. C. P. Clever to John V. Watts, December 28, 1855, Ritch Collection (Univ. of New Mexico, Albuquerque, N.M.), microfilm, roll 1.

21. "Note," December 5, 1855, Ritch Collection, microfilm, roll 4.

22. *Santa Fe Weekly Gazette,* May 27, 1860, New Mexico Territorial Papers, microfilm, roll 1.

23. Robert W. Johannsen, *Frontier Politics on the Eve of the Civil War* (Seattle, Wash.: Univ. of Washington Press, 1955), passim.

24. *Missouri Republican,* April 28, 1847.

25. Ibid., October 30, 1851.

26. Howard H. Lamar, *The Far Southwest* (New Haven, Conn.: Yale Univ. Press, 1966), pp. 102-3.

27. Ralph Emerson Twitchell, *The History of the Military Occupation of the Territory of New Mexico* (New York: Arno Press, 1976), pp. 387-89.

28. *Missouri Republican,* September 27, 1853.

29. William Carr Lane to William Glasgow, February 27, 1854, in Ralph P. Bieber, "Letters of William Carr Lane, 1852-1854," *New Mexico Historical Review,* 3 (1928), p. 201.

30. *Missouri Republican,* October 27, 1855.

31. Ibid.

32. Bishop Lamy to Archbishop Purcell, December 30, 1855, Lamy Papers (Univ. of Notre Dame, South Bend, Ind.), Letters.

33. "Election Results," New Mexico Territorial Papers, microfilm, roll 1.

34. Samuel Ellison to J. J. Webb, n.d., Ritch Collection, microfilm, roll 4.

35. *Santa Fe Weekly Gazette,* October 9, 1858.

36. Miguel Otero, *Address to the People of New Mexico* (Santa Fe, N.M.: n.p., 1860), p. 3.

37. Ibid., pp. 3-4.

Epilogue

1. *Santa Fe Weekly Gazette,* November 10, 1860, New Mexico Territorial Papers, National Archives (Univ. of Northern Iowa, Cedar Falls, Iowa), microfilm, roll 1.

2. Hubert H. Bancroft, *History of Arizona and New Mexico, 1550-1888* (San Francisco, Calif.: The History Company, 1889), p. 684; Samuel Ellison, "Interview with Edward H. Bergmann," Cimarron, N.M., 1882, Ritch Collection (Univ. of New Mexico, Albuquerque, N.M.), microfilm, roll 7.

3. Interview with Juan Ortega, August 10, 1969.

4. *Missouri Republican,* August 7, 1860.

5. Ibid., August 6, 1860.

6. Ellison, "Interview."

7. *Missouri Republican,* October 7, 1861.

8. Ibid., February 28, 1861.

9. Ibid., April 11, 1861.

10. Ellison, "Interview."

11. *Santa Fe Weekly Gazette,* May 11, 1861, New Mexico Territorial Papers, microfilm, roll 1.

12. *Missouri Republican,* passim, 1861.

13. Abraham Rencher to William H. Seward, April 14, 1861, New Mexico Territorial Papers, microfilm, roll 2.

14. Ibid., August 10, 1861.

15. Henry Connelly to William H. Seward, November 17, 1861, New Mexico Territorial Papers, microfilm, roll 2.

16. Interviews with Mexican-Americans, Santa Fe and Las Vegas, Summer, 1969, 1970; Fall 1971.

17. Brother Angelus Gabriel, *The Christian Brothers in the United States, 1848-1948* (New York: D. X. McMullen, 1948), pp. 472-77; Alvin R. Sunseri, "St. Michael's College," in *La Salle Auxiliary,* 39 (Spring, 1960), passim; J. R. Kelly, *History of the New Mexico Military Institute, 1891-1941* (Albuquerque, N.M.: Univ. of New Mexico Press, 1953), passim.

18. Interview with Dr. John M. Lucas, July 5, 1963.

19. Interview with Rodolfo "Corky" Gonzales, April 28, 1969.

20. Ibid.

21. Questionnaires submitted to students during Fall and Winter 1971-72 at College of Santa Fe, Santa Fe, N.M.; New Mexico Highlands University, Las Vegas, New Mexico.

22. Gonzales, interview.

23. William Madsen, *Mexican-American of South Texas* (New York: Holt, Rinehart and Winston, 1964), passim.

Glossary

ACEQUIA. Ditch which ran between two points of a river through which flowed water for irrigation purposes.

ALIANCISTA. A member of the Alianze Federal de Mercedes, Reies Tijerina's organization.

ANGLO. Short form of Anglo-American; in the Southwest sometimes designating all non-Mexican-descent Americans who are not of Indian descent.

AZLAN. Mythical homeland of the Aztec or Mexican Indians.

BARRIO. District; in the United States, Mexican-American quarter of town.

BRACERO. From Brazo, "arm"; a worker, a hired hand, especially a Mexican, brought to the United States under labor contract.

CALIFORNIO. Original Hispanic-Mexican inhabitant of California, or his descendant.

CHICANO. Truncated form of Mexicano, today with overtones of ethnic nationalism and activism.

COLONIA. Small settlement, sometimes part of a town, inhabited by Mexicans.

CONQUISTADOR(es). Early Spanish conquerors of the New World.

COYOTE (collote). One who is part Indian and part Spanish.

EMPRESARIO. Land-grantee who was required to bring in a specified number of settlers in order to validate his grant.

GENIZARO. An individual whose origin was unknown and generally considered from one of the tribes of the plains.

HIDALGO. A nobleman.

HISPANO. New Mexican of Hispanic-Mexican origins with emphasis on the Hispanic.

HOMBRE DE COLOR (Man of Color). A shade lighter than the mulatto and several generations removed from the marriage of a black and Spaniard.

LULAC. League of United Latin American Citizens, founded in 1929.

MESTIZAJE. Process of physical blending of Indian and European.

MESTIZO. Literally "mixed"; a person of European and Indian ancestry; or in New Mexico sometimes used to designate one who has in his lifetime arrived from Mexico.

MEXICANO. Usually a person from Mexico; also a person of Mexican descent in the United States Southwest.

MOJADO. Literally "wet"; one who enters the United States illegally, theoretically by swimming the Rio Grande River.

MULATTO. A person of European and African ancestry. Usually first generation.

NUEVO MEXICANO. Hispanic-Mexican inhabitant of area of New Mexico.

PATRON. Boss, patron; usually a large landowner.

PENITENTE. Member of a fanatical Catholic religious group in New Mexico.

PEON(es). Worker, usually tied to the land.

PRESIDIO. Military Fort.

PUEBLO. Township, village.

RANCHERO. Owner of a ranch; or related to ranching.

RANCHO. A rural property, often one on which cattle are raised.

LA RAZA. Ethnic term for Spanish-speaking people, connoting a spirit of belonging and a sense of common destiny.

LA RAZA UNIDA. Political party founded in 1970.

RICO. Literally a rich person; used in the Southwest to denote a member of the upper class.

SANGRIA. Secondary ditches in New Mexico that carried water from acequias to fields for irrigation purposes.

SOLAR(es). Lot for town house; also town house.

SURUMATO. Pejorative term, especially used in New Mexico, for Mexican; origin uncertain.

TEJANO. Hispanic-Mexican inhabitant of Texas area. In New Mexico often used in a pejorative sense when applied to Anglos from Texas.

TIO TACO. Chicano pejorative version of "Uncle Tom." Sometimes in New Mexico the terms Tio Tomes or Tio Tom are used instead.

VAQUERO. Mexican cowboy.

VENDIDO. "Sell-out," one who betrays la raza.

Notes on Sources

In examining the relations between Mexican-Americans and Anglo-Americans, I have relied heavily on publicly articulated observations made by Anglo-Americans, and to a lesser degree, by Mexican-Americans. I have also made extensive use of the newspapers published during this period, including the *Missouri Republican,* 1845-1861, a rich source of information used only sparingly in the past. The oral history technique was employed because the Mexican-Americans and Indians are great storytellers, with many families preserving an oral-history tradition. This method has been used with caution, however, for the writer accepted as historically valid only those observations that were supported by written evidence. The most important of these interviews were those with the following individuals: Harpur Vincentito, a Jicarilla Apache and occasional movie extra and advisor, who revealed a fascinating new world of New Mexican Indian lore and legend; Juan Ortega, Jose Naranjo, and Jose Martinez, three elderly New Mexicans having keen memories whose views, although embittered, were candid and deserving of critical evaluation; Rodolfo "Corky" Gonzales, interviewed by the writer during a press conference because his views best reflect those of the hundreds of Chicano students with whom the writer has spoken during the past decade; and finally, Judge Dean C. Mabry of Trinidad, Colorado, whose extensive knowledge of the relations between minority groups and Anglo-Americans in southern Colorado and northern New Mexico made him an important source of information on peonage and Indian slavery.

The storyteller tradition among Mexican-Americans and the necessity of understanding the feelings of Mexican-Americans today resulted in the utilization of the questionnaire method in an attempt to discover the reaction of the "insiders" to the Anglo-Americans. Thus, with the assistance of the University of Northern Iowa Social Research Center, questionnaires were prepared and distributed to students in northern New Mexico that partially resolved the problem of a lack of written evidence among the Mexican-Americans. Brother A. Raymond of the College of Santa Fe and James Angel of New Mexico Highlands University were of great help in completing this project.

In the more traditional method of historical research, extensive use was made not only of manuscript collections in Washington, D.C., and New Mexico, but also of the books and journals included in the bibliography.

Bibliography

Primary Sources

Manuscripts

National Archives, Washington, D.C.
Letters Received by the Office of Indian Affairs: New Mexico Superintendency, 1849–1861, Microfilm (Rolls 546-550), T-21.
Letters Sent to New Mexico by the Adjutant General's Office, 1845–1848, Microfilm (Roll 47), M-565.
New Mexico Territorial Papers, 1851–1861, Microfilm, T-17.

New Mexico State Records Center and Archives,
Santa Fe, New Mexico
Alvarez, Manuel, Papers, 1842–1856.
Constitutional Convention Papers, 1850.
Governors Papers, 1846–1861.
Miscellaneous Territorial Papers, 1851–1861.
Read, Benjamin M., Collection, 1846–1861.
Twitchell, Ralph Emerson, Papers, 1846–1861.
Vigil, Donaciano, Papers, 1846–1850.

Division of Manuscripts, Library of Congress
Fillmore, Millard, Papers, 1850.
McCall, George A., Papers, 1848–1850.
Taylor, Zachary, Papers, 1848–1850.

Special Collections Division, Zimmerman Library, University of New Mexico, Albuquerque, New Mexico
Otero, Miguel A., Papers, 1897.
Ritch, William G., Collection, 1846–1861, Microfilm (Rolls 1-7).

Separate Items
Cass, Lewis, Papers, 1848. William C. Clements Library of Americana, University of Michigan, Ann Arbor, Michigan.
Davis, W. W. H., Papers, 1853–1857. Beinecke Library of Rare Books and Manuscripts, Yale University, New Haven, Connecticut.
Ellison, Samuel. A History of New Mexico. Bancroft Library, University of California, Berkeley, California.
Lamy, Jean, Papers, 1853. Memorial Library, University of Notre Dame, South Bend, Indiana.
Seward, William H., Papers, 1850. Rush Rhewes Library, University of Rochester, Rochester, New York.

Government Documents

Congressional Globe, 1846–1861. Vol. [16], 1847; Vol. [17], 1848; Vol. [18], 1849; Vol. 21, 1850.
New Mexico. *Constitution, 1850.*
————. *House and Council Journals of the Territory of New Mexico, 1851–52.*
————. *Journals of the Executive Proceedings of the Territorial Assemblies, 1851–1853.*
————. *The Laws of the Assembly of New Mexico, 1847.*
————. *Laws of the Territory of New Mexico, 1847–1864.*
————. *Message of William Carr Lane, Governor of the Territory of New Mexico, to the Legislative Assembly of the Territory at Santa Fe, Dec. 7, 1852.*
————. "Organic Act Establishing the Territory of New Mexico: Approved September 30, 1850," *New Mexico Statutes Annotated.* Compiled and annotated by Stephen B. Davis, Jr., and Merritt C. Mecham. Denver, 1915.
————. *Organic Law of the Territory of New Mexico, 1846* (Kearny Code).
U. S. Bureau of Census. *Historical Statistics of the United States, Cotional Times to 1957.* Washington, D.C.: Government Printing Office, 1960.
U. S. House of Representatives. "California and New Mexico: Message from the President of the United States, Transmitting Information in

answer to a Resolution of the House on the 31st of December, 1849, on the Subject of California and New Mexico," Jan. 21, 1850. *House Ex. Doc.*, 31 Cong., 1 Sess., No. 17 (Serial 573), 976.

————. "Message from the President of the United States, Communicating in Compliance with a Resolution of the Senate, Information in Relation to Military Orders Issued to the United States Officers at Santa Fe," June 17, 1850. *House Ex. Doc.*, 31 Cong., 1 Sess., No. 56 (Serial 561), 15.

————. "Message from the President of the United States, in Answer to a Resolution of the Senate Calling for Information in Relation to the Formation of a State Government in New Mexico," July 1, 1850. *House Ex. Doc.*, 31 Cong., 1 Sess., No. 60, Parts 1 and 2 (Serial 561), 2.

————. "Message from the President of the United States, Transmitting a Copy of the Constitution of New Mexico, Together with a Digest of Votes for and Against It," Sept. 9, 1850. *House Ex. Doc.*, 31 Cong., 1 Sess., No. 74 (Serial 562), 17.

————. "Message from the President of the United States, in Reference to the Texas Boundary," Aug. 1, 1850. *House Ex. Doc.*, 31 Cong., 1 Sess., No. 82 (Serial 579), 1–5.

————. "Military and Indian Affairs in New Mexico," April 1, 1851. *House Ex. Doc.*, 32 Cong., 1 Sess., No. 2 (Serial 634), 125–26.

————. "Report on Military and Indian Affairs," March 13, 1851. *House Ex. Doc.*, 32 Cong., 1 Sess., No. 2 (Serial 634), 137–43.

Books

Albert, Lieutenant J. W. *Report of Lieutenant J. W. Abert of his examination of New Mexico in the years 1846–47.* Senate Ex. Doc. 23, 30 Cong., 1 Sess., Washington, 1848.

Baird, Spruce M. "Reports from a Texas Agent in New Mexico, 1849," in *New Spain and the Anglo-American West: Historical Contributions* (Presented to Herbert Eugene Bolton). Vol. II. Edited by W. C. Binkley. Los Angeles, California: Private Printing, 1932.

Baker, George E., ed. *The Works of William H. Seward.* Vol. I. New York: Redfield Press, 1855.

Bartlett, John Russell. *Personal Narrative of Explorations and Incidents in Texas, New Mexico, California, Sonora, and Chihuahua, Connected with the United States and Mexican Boundary Commission During the Years 1850, '51, '52 and '53.* 2 vols. New York: D. Appleton and Company, 1854. Reprint, Chicago: Regnery, 1965.

Benton, Thomas Hart. *Thirty Years' View: or, a History of the Working*

of the American Government for Thirty Years, from 1820 to 1850.
2 vols. New York: Appleton and Company, 1854-1856.

Blaine, James G. *Twenty Years of Congress: From Lincoln to Garfield.*
Vol. II. Norwich, Connecticut: The Henry Bill Publishing Company,
1884–1886.

Calhoun, James S. *The Official Correspondence of James S. Calhoun
While Indian Agent at Santa Fe and Superintendent of Indian Affairs
in New Mexico.* Edited by Annie Heloise Abel. Washington, D.C.:
Government Printing Office, 1915.

Clever, Charles P. *New Mexico, Her Necessities for Railroad Communication with the Atlantic and Pacific States.* Washington, D.C.,
1868.

Collins, J. L. *Answer to Certain Inflammatory Representations of R. H.
Weightman.* Santa Fe, New Mexico, 1852.

Davis, W. W. H. *El Gringo, or New Mexico and Her People.* 1857.
Reprint. Santa Fe, New Mexico: The Rydal Press, 1938.

Drum, Stella M., ed. *Down the Santa Fe Trail and into Mexico: The
Diary of Susan Shelby Magoffin, 1846–1847.* New Haven, Conn.:
Yale University Press, 1826.

Frazer, Robert W., ed. *Colonel George Archibald McCall, New Mexico
in 1850: a Military View.* Norman, Okla.: University of Oklahoma
Press, 1968.

Garrard, L. H. *Wah-to-Yah and the Taos Trail.* 1850. Reprint. Norman,
Okla.: University of Oklahoma Press, 1957.

Gibson, George Rutledge. *Journal of a Soldier under Kearny and Doniphan, 1846–1847.* Edited by Ralph P. Bieber. Glendale, Calif.:
Arthur H. Clark Company, 1935.

Gregg, Josiah. *Commerce of the Prairies.* Reprint from the edition of
1844. Edited by David Freeman Hawke. Indianapolis, Ind.: Bobbs-
Merrill, 1970.

Historical Society of New Mexico. *Journal of New Mexico Convention
of Delegates to Recommend a Plan of Civil Government* [,] *September, 1849.* No. 10. Santa Fe, N.M.: New Mexican Printing Company, 1910.

Hobbs, James. *Wild life in the Far West: Personal Adventures of a
Border Mountain Man. . . .* 1872. Reprint. Glorieto, N.M.: Rio
Grande Press, 1969.

Houghton, Joab. *Reply of Joab Houghton, Late Chief Justice of the
Supreme Court of the Temporary Civil Government of the Territory
of New Mexico, to the Personal and Slanderous Attack of R. H.
Weightman, in His Printed Pamphlet, Purporting to a "Speech"*

*Delivered in the House of Representatives on the 15th of March,
1852.* n.p., n.d.

Hughes, John Taylor. *Doniphan's Expedition Containing an Account of
the Conquest of New Mexico.* Cincinnati, Ohio: J. A. and J. V.
James, 1850.

Lange, Charles, and Riley, Carroll L., editors. *The Southwestern Journals of Adolph E. Bandelier, 1880–1882.* Albuquerque, N.M.: University of New Mexico Press, 1966.

Lummis, Charles F. *A Tramp Across the Continent.* New York: Charles
Scribner's Sons, 1898.

Mann, Horace. *Slavery: Letters and Speeches by Horace Mann.* Boston,
Mass.: B. B. Mussey and Company, 1853.

Moore, John Bassett, ed. *The Works of James Buchanan, Comprising
his Speeches, State Papers, and Private Correspondence.* Philadelphia,
Penn. and London, Eng.: J. B. Lippincott Company, 1908–11.

New Mexico Constitutional Convention Book. Denver, n.d.

Otero, Miguel A. *Address to the People of New Mexico.* Santa Fe,
N.M.: n.p., 1860.

———. *An Abolition Attack upon New Mexico, and a Reply by Hon.
M. A. Otero.* Santa Fe, N.M.: n.p., 1861.

———. *The Indian Depredations in the Territory of New Mexico.*
Washington, D.C.: n.p. 1859.

Otero, Miguel A. [Jr.] *My Nine Years as Governor of the Territory of
New Mexico.* Edited by Marion Dargah. Albuquerque, N.M.: University of New Mexico Press, 1940.

Phelps, John S. *Visit of Hon. John S. Phelps to New Mexico.* Quincy,
Ill.: n.p., 1859.

Pine, Pedro B. *Exposicion sucincta y sencilla de la provincia del Nueva
Mexico.* Cadiz, Spain: n.p., 1812.

Pope, John. *Report of Exploration of a Route for the Pacific Railroad,
near the 32nd Parallel of North Latitude from the Red River to the
Rio Grande. House Ex. Doc.* 929, 33 Cong., 1 Sess., Washington,
D.C., 1854.

Richardson, James D., comp. *A Compilation of the Messages and
Papers of the President, 1789–1902.* Washington, D.C.: Bureau
of National Literature and Art, 1903.

Ritch, William G., comp. *The Legislative Blue Book of the Territory of
New Mexico with the Rules of Order, Fundamental Law, Official
Register and Record, Historical Data, Compendium of Facts, etc., etc.*
Santa Fe, N.M.: Charles W. Green, Public Printer, 1882.

Russell, John T., comp. *Official Register N. M., Volunteers Called into*

Service of the United States, under the President's Proclamation of May 3, 1861. Santa Fe, N.M.: n.p., 1862.

Smith, Hugh N. *Address by Hugh N. Smith, of New Mexico to the People of that Territory.* Washington, D.C.: n.p., 1850.

Weightman, R. H. *Communication of R. H. Weightman. Senate Ex. Doc.* 76, 31 Cong., 1 Sess., Washington, D.C., 1850.

Newspapers

Capital (Santa Fe). Undated.

Denver Post, 1890, 1969.

Denver Republican, 1906–1909.

Las Vegas Daily Optic, 1898, 1963.

Missouri Republican (St. Louis), 1845–1861.

National Era (Washington), 1848.

The New Mexican (Santa Fe, New Mexico), 1849–1900, 1956-1970 (title varies and there are weekly as well as daily issues).

New York Daily Times, 1854–1860.

New York Herald, 1857–1860.

New York Tribune, 1846–1861.

Santa Fe Republican, 1847–1848.

Santa Fe Weekly Gazette, 1853–1861.

Secondary Sources

Books

Adams, Eleanor B., and Chavez, Fray Angelico. *The Missions of New Mexico, 1776: A Description by Fray Fransisco Atanasio Dominquez.* Albuquerque, N.M.: University of New Mexico Press, 1956.

An Illustrated History of New Mexico. Chicago, Ill.: Lewis Publishing Company, 1895.

Arnold, Elliott. *The Times of the Gringo.* New York: Knopf, 1953.

Arny, W. F. M. *Interesting Items Regarding New Mexico.* Santa Fe, N.M.: Manderfield and Tucker, Printers, 1872.

Bailey, L. R. *Indian Slave Trade in the Southwest.* Los Angeles, Calif.: Westernlore Press, 1966.

Bancroft, Frederic. *The Life of W. H. Seward.* 2 vols. New York: Harper and Brothers, 1900.

Bancroft, Hubert H. *The History of Arizona and New Mexico, 1530–1888.* San Francisco, Calif.: The History Company, Publishers, 1889.

Bandelier, Adolf F. *Final Report of Investigation among the Indians of the Southwestern United States.* Cambridge, Mass.: J. Wilson and Son, 1890.

Beck, Warren. *New Mexico: A History of Four Centuries.* Norman, Okla.: University of Oklahoma Press, 1962.

Bender, Averam B. *The March of Empire: Frontier Defense in the Southwest, 1848–1860.* Lawrence, Kan.: University of Kansas Press, 1952.

Binkley, William Campbell. *The Expansionist Movement in Texas, 1836–1850,* Vol. 13. Berkeley, Calif.: University of California Publications in History, 1925.

Blackmar, Frank W. *Spanish Institutions of the Southwest.* Baltimore, Md.: The Johns Hopkins Press, 1891.

Bloom, Lansing B., and Donnelly, Thomas C. *New Mexico History and Civics.* Albuquerque, N.M.: University of New Mexico Press, 1933.

Bolton, Herbert E. *The Spanish Borderlands.* New Haven, Conn.: Yale University Press, 1921.

Brayer, Herbert O., and Blackmore, William. *The Spanish-Mexican Land Grants of New Mexico and Colorado, 1863–1878: A Case Study in the Economic Development of the West.* Vol. I. Denver, Colo.: Bradford-Robinson Press, 1949.

————. *Pueblo Indian Land Grants of the Rio Abajo, New Mexico.* Albuquerque, N.M.: University of New Mexico Press, 1939.

Burma, John H. *Spanish-Speaking Groups in the United States.* Durham, N.C.: Duke University Press, 1954.

Carrol, Bailey, and Haggard, J. Villasana. *Three New Mexico Chronicles: The Exposition of Don Pedro Bautista Pino, 1812; The Ojeada of Lic Antonio Barreiro, 1832, and the Additions by Don Jose Agustin de Escudero, 1849.* Albuquerque, N.M.: University of New Mexico Press, 1942.

Cather, Willa. *Death Comes for the Archbishop.* New York: Knopf, 1927.

Chavez, Fray Angelico, comp. *Archives of the Archdiocese of Santa Fe, 1678–1900.* Washington, D.C.: Academy of American Franciscan History, 1957.

————. *Origins of New Mexican Families.* Santa Fe, N.M.: Historical Society of New Mexico, 1954.

Clarke, Dwight. *Stephen Watts Kearny: Soldier of the West.* Norman, Okla.: University of Oklahoma Press, 1961.

Cleland, Robert Glass. *This Reckless Breed of Men: The Trappers and Furtraders of the Southwest.* New York: Knopf, 1952.

Coan, Charles. *A History of New Mexico*. Chicago and New York: The American Historical Society, Inc., 1925.

Colton, Ray C. *The Civil War in the Western Territories: Arizona, Colorado, New Mexico, and Utah*. Norman, Okla.: University of Oklahoma Press, 1959.

Davis, Ellis Arthur, ed. *The Historical Encyclopedia of New Mexico*. 2 vols. Albuquerque, N.M.: University of New Mexico Press, 1945.

Diaz, Albert James. *A Guide to the Microfilm of Papers Relating to New Mexico Land Grants*. Albuquerque, N.M.: University of New Mexico Press, 1960.

Donnelly, Thomas C. *The Story of New Mexico, Its History and Its Government*. Albuquerque, N.M.: University of New Mexico Press, 1937.

Duffus, R. L. *The Santa Fe Trail*. New York: Tudor Publishing Company, 1930.

Dunn, J. P. *Massacres of the Mountains*. New York: Archer House (distributed by Herman and Stephens), 1958.

Emmett, Chris. *Fort Union and the Winning of the Southwest*. Norman, Okla.: University of Oklahoma Press, 1965.

Estergreen, M. Morgan. *Kit Carson: A Portrait in Courage*. Norman, Okla.: University of Oklahoma Press, 1962.

Faulk, Odie. *Land of Many Frontiers: A History of the American Southwest*. New York: Oxford University Press, 1968.

Fergusson, Erna. *New Mexico: A Pageant of Three Peoples*. New York: Knopf, 1951.

Finlay, J. R. *Report of Appraisal of Mining Properties of New Mexico*. Santa Fe, N.M.: Printed at the Catholic Publication Company, 1922.

Frost, John. *The Mexican War and Its Warriors; Comprising a Complete History of All the Operations of the American Armies in Mexico. . . .* New Haven, Conn.: Yale University Press, 1949.

Gabriel, Brother Angelus. *The Christian Brothers in the United States, 1848–1948*. New York: D. X. McMullen Company, 1948.

Ganaway, Loomis M. *New Mexico and the Sectional Controversy*. Albuquerque, N.M.: University of New Mexico Press, 1944.

Garber, Paul Neff. *The Gadsden Treaty*. Philadelphia, Penn.: Press of the University of Pennsylvania, 1923.

Glick, Thomas F. *Irrigation and Society in Medieval Valencia*. Cambridge, Mass.: Harvard University Press, 1970.

Gonzalez, Nancie L. *The Spanish-Americans of New Mexico*. Albuquerque, N.M.: University of New Mexico Press, 1967.

Grivas, Theodore. *Military Governments in California, 1846–1850:*

With a Chapter on Their Prior Use in Louisiana, Florida, and New Mexico. Glendale, Calif.: Arthur H. Clark Company, 1963.

Haines, Helen. *History of New Mexico . . . , 1530–1890.* New York: New Mexico Historical Publishing Company, 1891.

Hall, Frank. *History of the State of Colorado.* 4 vols. Chicago, Ill.: Blakely Printing Company, 1888–1895.

Hall, Martin H. *Sibley's New Mexico Campaign.* Austin, Tex.: University of Texas Press, 1960.

Hayes, A. A. *New Colorado and the Santa Fe Trail.* New York: Harper and Brothers, 1880.

Heitman, Francis B. *Historical Register and Dictionary of the United States Army, From Its Organization, September 29, 1789, to March 2, 1903.* Washington, D.C.: Government Printing Office, 1903.

Heyman, Max L. *Prudent Soldier: A Biography of Major General E. R. S. Canby, 1813–1873.* Glendale, Calif.: Arthur H. Clark Company, 1959.

Horgan, Paul. *Great River.* 2 vols. New York: Rinehart, 1954.

Horn, Calvin. *New Mexico's Troubled Years: The Story of the Early Territorial Governors.* Albuquerque, N.M.: Horn and Wallace, 1963.

Hunt, Aurora. *Major General James Henry Carleton, 1814–1873.* Glendale, Calif.: Arthur H. Clark Company, 1953.

————. *Judge Kirby Benedict.* Glendale, Calif.: Arthur H. Clark Company, 1961.

Inman, Henry. *The Old Santa Fe Trail; The Story of a Great Highway.* 1897. Reprint. Minneapolis, Minn.: Ross and Haines, 1966.

Irion, Frederick C. *Selected and Annotated Bibliography on Politics in New Mexico.* Santa Fe, N.M.: Legislative Council Service of New Mexico, 1959.

Jackson, W. Turrentine. *Wagon Roads West.* New Haven, Conn.: Yale University Press, 1965.

James, Harold Lloyd. *The Santa Fe Trail.* Reprint. Globe, Ariz.: Southwestern Monuments Association, 1968.

Jaramillo, Cleofas. *Shadows of the Past.* Santa Fe, N.M.: n.p., 1941.

Jenkins, Myra Ellen, and Schroeder, Albert H. *A Brief History of New Mexico.* Albuquerque, N.M.: University of New Mexico Press, 1974.

Johannsen, Robert W. *Frontier Politics on the Eve of the Civil War.* Seattle, Wash.: University of Washington Press, 1955.

Keleher, William A. *Turmoil in New Mexico, 1846–1868.* Santa Fe, N.M.: Rydal Press, 1952.

Kelly, J. R. *History of the New Mexico Military Institute, 1891–1941.* Albuquerque, N.M.: University of New Mexico Press, 1953.

Lamar, Howard R. *The Far Southwest, 1846–1912: A Territorial History*. New Haven, Conn.: Yale University Press, 1966.

Larson, Robert W. *New Mexico's Quest for Statehood, 1846–1912*. Albuquerque, N.M.: University of New Mexico Press, 1968.

Lavender, David. *Bent's Fort*. Garden City, N.Y.: Doubleday, 1952.

Loomis, Noel M. *The Texan-Santa Fe Pioneers*. Norman, Okla.: University of Oklahoma Press, 1958.

McCormac, Eugene Irving. *James K. Polk, a Political Biography*. Berkeley, Calif.: University of California Press, 1922.

McWilliams, Carey. *North From Mexico: The Spanish-Speaking People of the United States*. 1949. Reprint. New York: Greenwood Press, 1968.

Madsen, William. *Mexican-Americans of South Texas*. New York: Holt, Rinehart and Winston, 1964.

Moorhead, Max L. *New Mexico's Royal Road: Trade and Travel on the Chihuahua Trail*. Norman, Okla.: University of Oklahoma Press, 1958.

Napton, William Barclay. *Over the Santa Fe Trail, 1857*. 1905. Reprint. Santa Fe, N.M.: Stagecoach Press, 1964.

Nevins, Allan. *Ordeal of the Union: Fruits of Manifest Destiny, 1847–1852*. New York: Charles Scribner's Sons, 1947.

Oliva, Leo E. *Soldiers on the Santa Fe Trail*. Norman, Okla.: University of Oklahoma Press, 1967.

Paul, Rodman W. *The Mining Frontiers of the Far West, 1848–1880*. New York: Holt, Rinehart and Winston, 1963.

Perrigo, Lynn. *Our Spanish Southwest*. Dallas, Tex.: B. Upshaw, 1960.

——————. *The American Southwest: Its Peoples and Cultures*. New York: Holt, Rinehart and Winston, 1971.

Peters, Dewitt C. *Kit Carson's Life and Adventures from Facts Narrated by Himself*. Hartford, Conn.: Gilman and Company, 1874.

——————. *The Life and Adventures of Kit Carson*. New York: W. R. C. Clark and Company, 1858.

Pettis, George H. *The California Column*. Santa Fe, N.M.: New Mexico Printing Company, 1908.

Pitt, Leonard. *The Decline of the Californios: A Social History of the Spanish-Speaking Californians, 1846–1900*. Berkeley, Calif.: University of California Press, 1966.

Prince, L. Bradford. *A Concise History of New Mexico*. Cedar Rapids, Iowa: Torch Press, 1912.

Rayback, Robert J. *Millard Fillmore: Biography of a President*. Buffalo, N.Y.: H. Stewart, 1925.

Read, Benjamin M. *Illustrated History of New Mexico*. Santa Fe, N.M.: New Mexico Printing Company, 1912.

Rippy, J. Fred. *The United States and Mexico*. New York: A. A. Knopf, 1926.

Rister, Carl Coke. *The Southwestern Frontier*. Glendale, Calif.: Arthur H. Clark Company, 1928.

Ritch, W. G. *Aztlan, the History of New Mexico*. Boston, Mass.: D. Lathrop and Company, 1885.

————. *Inaugural Address of the President of the Historical Society of New Mexico*. Santa Fe, N.M.: New Mexico Book and Job Printing Department, 1881.

Sabin, Edwin L. *Kit Carson Days, 1809–1868*. 1914. Reprint. New York: Press of the Pioneers, 1935.

Sacks, B. *Be It Enacted: The Creation of the Territory of Arizona*. Phoenix, Ariz.: Arizona Historical Foundation, 1964.

Sanchez, George I. *Forgotten People: A Study of New Mexicans*. Albuquerque, N.M.: University of New Mexico Press, 1940.

Saunders, Lyle. *A Guide to Materials Bearing on Cultural Relations in New Mexico*. Albuquerque, N.M.: University of New Mexico Press, 1944.

Schroeder, Albert H., ed. *The Changing Ways of Southwestern Indians*. Albuquerque, N.M.: University of New Mexico Press, 1973.

Smith, Justin H. *The War With Mexico*. 2 vols. New York: Macmillan, 1919.

Spicer, Edward E. *Cycles of Conquest: The Impact of Spain, Mexico, and the United States on the Indians of the Southwest, 1533–1960*. Tucson, Ariz.: University of Arizona Press, 1962.

Taylor, William Robert. *Cavalier and Yankee*. London, Eng.: W. H. Allen, 1961.

Thomas, David Yancey. *A History of Military Government of the Newly Acquired Territory of the United States*. 1904. Reprint. New York: A M S Press Edition, 1967.

Trennert, Robert A. *Alternative to Extinction: Federal Indian Policy and the Beginning of the Reservation System, 1846–51*. Philadelphia, Penn.: Temple University Press, 1975.

Twitchell, Ralph Emerson. *Historical Sketch of Governor William Carr Lane*. Santa Fe, N.M.: Historical Society of New Mexico, 1917.

————. *The History of the Military Occupation of the Territory of New Mexico*. 1909. Reprint. New York: Arno Press, 1976.

————. *The Leading Facts of New Mexican History*. 2 vols. Cedar Rapids, Iowa: Torch Press, 1912.

————. *The Spanish Archives of New Mexico.* Cedar Rapids, Iowa: Torch Press, 1914.

————. *The Story of the Conquest of Santa Fe, New Mexico, and the Building of Old Fort March.* Santa Fe, N.M.: Historical Society of New Mexico, 1923.

————. *Old Santa Fe: The Story of New Mexico's Ancient Capital.* 1925. Reprint. Glorieta, N.M.: Rio Grande Press, 1963.

Utley, Robert M. *Frontiersmen in Blue: The United States Army and the Indian, 1848–1865.* New York: Macmillan, 1967.

Valdez, C. *Compiled Laws of New Mexico in 1885.* Topeka, Kan.: n.p., 1885.

Vestal, Stanley. *The Old Santa Fe Trail.* Boston, Mass.: Houghton Mifflin Company, 1939.

Vigil, Jose. *Jose de la Crus Vigil vs. the Mescalero Apache Indians.* Santa Fe, N.M.: n.p., n.d.

Wagner, Henry R. *The Spanish Southwest, 1542–1794.* 2 vols. Albuquerque, N.M.: University of New Mexico Press, 1937.

Watt, W. Montgomery. *A History of Islamic Spain.* Chicago, Illinois: Aldine Publishing Co., 1967.

Wayner, Louis H. *Archbishop Lamy, an Epoch Maker.* Santa Fe, N.M.: Santa Fe New Mexican Publishing Corporation, 1936.

Weber, David J., ed. *Foreigners in Their Native Land: Historical Roots of the Mexican-Americans.* Albuquerque, N.M.: University of New Mexico Press, 1973.

Westphall, Victor. *The Public Domain in New Mexico, 1854–1891.* Albuquerque, N.M.: University of New Mexico Press, 1965.

Wittfogel, Karl A. *Oriental Despotism: Hydraulic Society.* New Haven, Conn.: Yale University Press, 1957.

Articles

Abel, Annie H. "The Journal of John Greiner." *Old Santa Fe* 3 (1916): 189–243.

————, ed. "Indian Affairs in New Mexico under the Administration of William Carr Lane: From the Journal of John Ward." *New Mexico Historical Review* 16 (1941): 206–232, 328–358.

Amsden, Charles. "The Navajo Exile at Bosque Redondo." *New Mexico Historical Review* 8 (1933): 31–50.

Anderson, Hattie M. "Mining and Indian Fighting in Arizona and New Mexico, 1853–61." *Panhandle-Plains Historical Review* 1 (1928): 67–115.

Anderson, Latham. "Canby's Campaign in New Mexico, 1861." *Magazine of History* 3 (1906): 141–148.
Anonymous. "The Conquest of Santa Fe." *El Palacio* 13 (1922): 152–54.
———. "Early Commerce with Santa Fe." *Santa Fe Magazine* 4 (1910): 29–32.
Atherton, Lewis E. "Disorganizing effects of the Mexican War on the Santa Fe Trade." *Kansas Historical Quarterly* 11 (1937): 115–123.
Baldwin, P. M. "A Historical Note on the Boundaries of New Mexico." *New Mexico Historical Review* 5 (1930): 117–137.
———. "A Short History of the Mesilla Valley." *New Mexico Historical Review* 13 (1938): 314–19.
Baur, John E. "The Health Seekers in the Westward Movement, 1830–1900." *Mississippi Valley Historical Review* 46 (1959): 91–110.
Beers, Henry P. "Military Protection of the Santa Fe Trail to 1843." *New Mexico Historical Review* 12 (1937): 113–133.
Bender, A. B. "Frontier Defense in the Territory of New Mexico, 1846–1853." *New Mexico Historical Review* 9 (1934): 249–272.
———. "Government Explorations in the Territory of New Mexico, 1846–1859." *New Mexico Historical Review* 9 (1934): 1–32.
———. "Military Transportation in the Southwest, 1848–1860." *New Mexico Historical Review* 32 (1957): pp. 123–150.
Bieber, Ralph P. "Some Aspects of the Santa Fe Trail, 1848–1880." *Missouri Historical Review* 18 (1924): 158–166.
———. "The Southwestern Trails to California in 1849." *Mississippi Valley Historical Review* 12 (1925): 342–375.
———, ed. "Letters of William Carr Lane, 1852–1854." *New Mexico Historical Review* 3 (1928): 179–203.
Binkley, William Campbell. "New Mexico and the Texas–Santa Fe Expedition." *Southwestern Historical Quarterly* 27 (1923): 85–109.
———. "The Question of Texan Jurisdiction in New Mexico under the United States, 1848–1850." *Southwestern Historical Quarterly* 24 (1920): 1–38.
Bloom, Lansing B. "Beginnings of Representative Government in New Mexico." *New Mexico Historical Review* 21 (1946): 127–134.
———. "The Governors of New Mexico." *New Mexico Historical Review* 10 (1935): 152–157.
———. "New Mexico Under Mexican Administration, 1821–1846." *Old Santa Fe* 2 (1915): 351–380.
———, ed. "A Group of Kearny Letters." *New Mexico Historical Review* 5 (1930): 17–37.

Bolton, Herbert E. "The Mission as a Frontier Institution in the Spanish-American Colonies." *American Historical Review* 23 (1917): 42–61.

Bourne, Edward G. "The United States and Mexico, 1847–1848." *American Historical Review* 5 (1899): 491–502.

Bowden, J. J. "The Texas–New Mexico Boundary Dispute Along the Rio Grande." *Southwestern Historical Quarterly* 63 (1959): 221–237.

Brooks, Clinton E., and Reeve, Frank D., eds. "James Augustus Bennett, Forts and Forays . . . a Dragoon in New Mexico, 1850–1856," *New Mexico Historical Review* 22 (1947): 51–97, 140–176.

Burton, E. B. "Volunteer Soldiers of New Mexico." *Old Santa Fe* 1 (1913–1914): 386–419.

Carson, William G. B., ed. "William Carr Lane, Diary." *New Mexico Historical Review* 39 (1964): 181–234, 274–332.

Cheetham, Francis T. "The First Term of the American Court in Taos, New Mexico." *New Mexico Historical Review* 1 (1926): 23–41.

————. "Kit Carson, Pathbreaker, Patriot, and Humanitarian." *New Mexico Historical Review* 1 (1926): 375–399.

Connelley, William E., ed. "A Journal of the Santa Fe Trail." *Mississippi Valley Historical Review* 21 (1925): 72-98, 227-255.

Culmer, Frederic A. "Marking the Santa Fe Trail." *New Mexico Historical Review* 9 (1934): 79–93.

Curtis, F. S., Jr. "Influence of Weapons on New Mexican History." *New Mexico Historical Review* 1 (1926): 324–334.

Donnell, F. S. "The Confederate Territory of Arizona, as Compiled from Official Sources." *New Mexico Historical Review* 17 (1942): 148–163.

————. "When Las Vegas Was the Capital of New Mexico." *New Mexico Historical Review* 8 (1933): 265–272.

————. "When Texas Owned New Mexico to the Rio Grande." *New Mexico Historical Review* 8 (1933): 265–275.

Eaton, W. Clement. "Frontier Life in Southern Arizona, 1858–1861." *Southwestern Historical Quarterly* 37 (1933): 173–192.

Francis, E. K. "Padre Martinez: A New Mexican Myth." *New Mexico Historical Review* 21 (1956): 265–289.

Fuller, John D. P. "The Slavery Question and the Movement to Acquire Mexico, 1846–1848." *Mississippi Valley Historical Review* 21 (1934): 34–48.

Ganaway, Loomis Morton. "New Mexico and the Sectional Controversy, 1846–1861." *New Mexico Historical Review* 18 (1943): 113–47, 204–246, 325–348.

Goodrich, James W. "Revolt at Mora, 1847." *New Mexico Historical Review* 47 (1972): 49–60.

Gorman, Mrs. Samuel. "Samuel Gorman." *Old Santa Fe* 1 (1913–1914): 308–311.

Greer, Richard R. "Origins of the Foreign-Born Population of New Mexico during the Territorial Period." *New Mexico Historical Review* 17 (1942): 281–287.

Hamilton, Holman. "Democratic Senate Leadership and the Compromise of 1850." *Mississippi Valley Historical Review* 41 (1954): 408, 411–413.

Harvey, Charles M. "The Story of the Santa Fe Trail." *Atlantic* 104 (1909): 774–785.

Hodder, F. H. "The Authorship of the Compromise of 1850." *Mississippi Valley Historical Review* 22 (1935): 525–536.

Hutchins, Wells A. "The Community Acequia: Its Origin and Development." *Southwestern Historical Quarterly* 31 (1927): 261–284.

Jones, Charles Irving, ed. "William Kronig, New Mexico Pioneer from his Memories of 1849–1860." *New Mexico Historical Review* 19, (1944): 185–224, 271–311.

Julian, George W. "Land-Stealing in New Mexico." *North American Review* CXLV (1887): 17–31.

Keleher, William A. "The Year of Decision." *New Mexico Historical Review* 22 (1947): 8–17.

Lamar, Howard R. "Political Patterns in New Mexico and Utah Territories, 1850–1900." *Utah Historical Review* 27 (1960): 363–387.

Larson, Robert W. "Statehood for New Mexico, 1888–1912." *New Mexico Historical Review* 37 (1962): 161–200.

Laumbach, Verna. "Las Vegas Before 1850." *New Mexico Historical Review* 8 (1933): 241–264.

Lindgren, Raymond E., ed. "A Diary of Kit Carson's Navajo Campaign." *New Mexico Historical Review* 21 (1946): 226–246.

Loyola, Sister Mary. "The American Occupation of New Mexico, 1821–1852." *New Mexico Historical Review* 14 (1939): 34–75, 143–199, 230–286.

McMurtrie, Douglas C. "The History of Early Printing in New Mexico, with Bibliography of the Known Issues of the Mexican Press, 1834–1860." *New Mexico Historical Review* 4 (1929): 372–410.

————. "Some Supplementary New Mexican Imprints, 1850–1860."
New Mexico Historical Review 7 (1932): 165–175.

McNitt, Frank. "Navajo Campaign and the Occupation of New Mexico,
1847–1848." *New Mexico Historical Review* 18 (1968): 173–194.

Marshall, Thomas M. "Commercial Aspects of the Texas–Santa Fe
Expedition." *Southwestern Historical Quarterly* 20 (1917): 242–259.

Moody, Marshall D. "Kit Carson, Agent to the Indians in New Mexico,
1853–1861." *New Mexico Historical Review* 28 (1953): 1–20.

Moorhead, Max L. "Spanish Transportation in the Southwest, 1540–
1846." *New Mexico Historical Review* 32 (1957): 107–122.

Murphy, Lawrence B. "The United States Army in Taos, 1847–1852."
New Mexico Historical Review 47 (1972): 33–41.

Noggle, Burl. "Anglo Observers of the Southwest Borderlands, 1825–
1890: The Rise of a Concept." *Arizona and the West* 1 (1959):
105–131.

Ogle, Ralph H. "Federal Control of the Western Apaches, 1848–1886."
New Mexico Historical Review 14 (1939): 309–365.

Parish, William J. "The German Jew and the Commercial Revolution in
Territorial New Mexico, 1850–1900." *New Mexico Historical Review*
35 (1960): 1–29, 129–150.

Perrigo, Lynn I. "New Mexico in the Mexican Period, as Revealed in
the Torres Documents," *New Mexico Historical Review* 29 (1954):
28–40.

Perrine, Fred S. "Military Escorts on the Santa Fe Trail." *New Mexico
Historical Review* 2 (1927): 175–193, 269–304.

————. "Uncle Sam's Camel Corps." *New Mexico Historical Review*
1 (1926): 434–444.

Poldervaart, Arie. "Black-Robed Justice in New Mexico, 1846–1912."
New Mexico Historical Review 22 (1947): 18–50, 109–139, 286–
314, 351–388; 23 (1949): 40–57, 129–145, 225–239.

Ramsdell, Chas W. "The Natural Limits of Slavery Expansion." *Mississippi Valley Historical Review* 16 (1929): 151–171.

Reeve, Frank D. "Federal Indian Policy in New Mexico, 1858–1880."
New Mexico Historical Review 12 (1937): 218–269.

Rippy, J. Fred. "Anglo-American Filibusters and the Gadsden Treaty."
Hispanic American Historical Review 5 (1922): 155–180.

————. "Boundary of New Mexico and the Gadsden Treaty." *Hispanic American Historical Review* 9 (1921): 715–742.

————. "The Indians of the Southwest in the Diplomacy of the United
States and Mexico, 1848–1853." *Hispanic American Historical Review* 2 (1919): 363–396.

————. "The Negotiation of the Gadsden Treaty." *Southwestern Historical Quarterly* 27 (1923): 1–26.

————. "A Ray of Light on the Gadsden Treaty." *Southwestern Historical Quarterly* 24 (1920–1921): 234–242.

Roberts, B. H. "The Mormon Battalion: its History and Achievements." *Deseret News* (1919): 12–16.

Shelton, Wilma Loy, comp. "Checklist of New Mexico Publications." *New Mexico Historical Review* 24 (1949): 130–155.

Simmons, Marc. "Spanish Irrigation Practices in New Mexico." *New Mexico Historical Review* 47 (1972): 135–151.

Spiegelberg, Flora. "Tribute to Archbishop Lamy of New Mexico." *El Palacio* 36 (1934): 22–25.

Spillman, W. J. "Adjustment of the Texas Boundary in 1850." *Southwestern Historical Quarterly* 7 (1904): 177–195.

Sunseri, Alvin R. "The Ludlow Massacre: A Study in the Mis-employment of the National Guard." *American Chronicle* 1 (1972): 21–28.

————. "St. Michael's College." *La Salle Auxiliary* 39 (1960): 24–25.

Taylor, Mendell Lee. "The Western Services of Stephen Watts Kearny, 1815–1848." *New Mexico Historical Review* 21 (1946): 169–184.

Tittmann, Edward D. "The Last Legal Frontier." *New Mexico Historical Review* 2 (1927): 219–227.

Townley, John. "The New Mexico Mining Company." *New Mexico Historical Review* 46 (January 1971): 57–73.

Twitchell, R. E. "Chief Justice Kirby Benedict." *Old Santa Fe* 1 (1913–1914): 49–92.

Van Cleave, Evret. "Credit on the Santa Fe Trail: Business Pioneering in Pueblo Regions." *Credit and Financial Management* 41 (1939): 16–17.

Walker, Charles S. "Causes of the Confederate Invasion of New Mexico." *New Mexico Historical Review* 8 (1933): 76–97.

Warner, Louis H. "Conveyance of Property, the Spanish and Mexican Way." *New Mexico Historical Review* 6 (1931): 334–359.

Westphall, Victor. "The Public Domain in New Mexico, 1854–1891." *New Mexico Historical Review* 33 (1958): 24–29, 37–39.

Wharton, Clarence. "Spruce McCoy Baird," *New Mexico Historical Review* 27 (1952): 300–314.

Wyman, Walker D. "The Military Phase of Santa Fe Freighting, 1846–1865." *Kansas Historical Quarterly* 1 (1931)' 415–428.

————. "F. X. Aubry, Santa Fe Freighter, Pathfinder, and Explorer." *New Mexico Historical Review* 12 (January 1932): 1-31.

Unpublished Dissertations and Theses

Avant, Louis. "The History of Catholic Education in New Mexico since the American Occupation." Master's thesis, University of New Mexico, 1940.

Carnes, Sister Mary Loyola. "The American Occupation of New Mexico." Ph.D. dissertation, University of California, 1922.

Caughey, John W. "Early Federal Relations with New Mexico." Master's thesis, University of California, Berkeley, 1926.

Ganaway, Loomis Morton. "New Mexico and the Sectional Controversy." Ph.D. dissertation, Vanderbilt University, 1941.

Grant, N. A. "A History of the Texas Boundary Disputes." Master's thesis, Colorado State Teachers College, 1930.

Helpler, Robert D. "William Watts Hart Davis in New Mexico." Master's thesis, University of New Mexico, 1941.

McLaughlin, Thomas J. "History of Fort Union, New Mexico." Master's thesis, University of New Mexico, 1952.

Mayfield, Thomas J., Jr. "The Development of the Public Schools in New Mexico Between 1848 and 1900." Master's thesis, University of New Mexico, 1938.

Reiter, Robert Louis. "The History of Fort Union, New Mexico," Ph.D. dissertation, University of California, Berkeley, 1953.

Stapleton, Ernest S. "The History of the Baptist Missions in New Mexico, 1849–1860." Master's thesis, University of New Mexico, 1954.

Tyler, Daniel. "New Mexico in the 1820's: The First Administration of Manuel Armijo." Ph.D. dissertation, University of New Mexico, 1970.

Interviews

Gonzales, Rodolfo "Corky." Personal Interview, Denver, Colorado. April 28, 1969.

Lucas, John. Personal Interview, New Mexico State Hospital, Las Vegas, New Mexico. July 5, 1963.

Mabry, Dean. Personal Interview, Trinidad, Colorado. January 30, 1969.

Martinez, Jose. Personal Interviews, Santa Fe, New Mexico. August 13, 1970. August 14, 1971.

Naranjo, Jose. Personal Interview, Santa Fe, New Mexico. August 10, 1969.

Ortega, Juan. Personal Interview, Santa Fe, New Mexico. August 10, 1969.

Vincentito, Harpur (Jicarilla Apache). Personal Interview, Santa Fe, New Mexico. August 9, 1969.

Questionnaire

Questionnaire entitled, "Reaction of the Mexican-Americans to the Anglo-American Occupation," 1971–1972. Compiled by the University of Northern Iowa Social Research Center, Cedar Falls, Iowa.

Index

ABOUT THE AUTHOR

Alvin R. Sunseri is professor of history, University of Northern Iowa at Cedar Falls, specializing in the history of wars, revolutions, and minorities. He received his Ph.D. in history from Louisiana State University. He has taught at the New Mexico Military Institute, the College of Santa Fe, the New Mexico Highlands University, and Western State University of Colorado. His work has been published in *The Journal of Mexican American History*, *Agricultural History*, *The Indian Historian*, *El Palacio*, and *The Negro History Bulletin*. He is a member of the American Historical Association, Organization of American Historians, and Southern Historical Association.